RECIPROCITY, INCORPORATED

The Little Business Book
of
Doing Well by Doing Good

by

Augie Nieto

INFINITY
PUBLISHING.COM

Copyright © 2010 by Augie Nieto

ISBN 0-7414-5618-4

Published by:

INFI∞ITY
PUBLISHING.COM

1094 New DeHaven Street, Suite 100
West Conshohocken, PA 19428-2713
Info@buybooksontheweb.com
www.buybooksontheweb.com
Toll-free (877) BUY BOOK
Local Phone (610) 941-9999
Fax (610) 941-9959

Printed in the United States of America

Published April 2010

Foreword

by Lance Armstrong

Augie Nieto and I are a lot alike.

Both of us grew up with difficulty and incomplete families. I've never met my birth father, but my single-parent mom worked to keep me out of trouble, which seemed to draw me like a magnet. Augie struggled with being overweight and lost his Mom before his senior year of high school. We used our troubled childhood experiences as a catapult to move forward, motivated to strive for more and to reach the top.

Both of us are completely into fitness and training... me with my bike racing and endurance training, and Augie working out and selling his Life Cycle stationary bikes as founder of Life Fitness, Inc., and now as Chairman of Octane Fitness.

Both of us have been struck down with the surprise diagnosis of tragic and debilitating "orphan" diseases that rarely strike. I fought against Stage III Testicular Cancer that had spread to my lungs, brain, and abdomen. Augie has Amyotrophic Lateral Sclerosis (ALS), more commonly known as Lou Gehrig's disease, which now continues to rob him of physical abilities.

Both of us have immersed ourselves into philanthropy for our causes… LiveStrong Foundation raises awareness and funds for curing cancer. The Augie's Quest Foundation supports a fast-track lab with the coordination of global ALS testing. Our determination to beat these diseases has already led to major overhauls in the way research is conducted and patients are treated.

Both of us have written autobiographies, chronicled our stories, and do everything we can to champion our causes. *It's Not About the Bike* was published in 2000 and *Augie's Quest* in 2007.

And I'm hoping against all odds that we will remain alike in one more way… that we will <u>both</u> be riding our bikes again.

Twenty years before I was diagnosed, testicular cancer was a death sentence. Everyone died. Nobody made it. And then almost overnight, it became one of the greatest oncology success stories when an Indiana doctor tested an experimental drug containing platinum. That same metal used to make your watch or wedding band saved my life. I'm living proof of this miraculous shift in medicine and I want the same for my friend.

Numerous similarities… but *Reciprocity Incorporated* is where we part ways and the difference becomes apparent. I am humbled by the brilliant observations and succinct compilation of life's most profound lessons shared in Augie's book. His storytelling and interviews with American leaders are inspirational — and the creation of this book is an unprecedented feat, unmatched in effort even by my own grueling Tour de France races. Augie interviewed from his wheelchair using voice-enhanced software and wrote each word using the big toe of his right foot to guide a mouse-ball, painstakingly selecting every letter in every insightful sentence.

For Augie, this is a work not only of genius, but of guts.

Augie: I honor you, my friend, for your incredible fortitude and for caring enough about those of us who are still in the process of learning these life lessons. You devoted the time, letter by letter, and wrote this book for all of us. Heartfelt thanks, buddy. Don't ever give up. You are my Chief Inspirational Officer.

Always Be Closing?

I started my first business as a sophomore in college, goaded into it by my economics professor. When he gave me a low C on a paper I'd written — a business plan for a health club — I told him I'd open one up and earn more than he did in a year's time. I leased retail space near our Claremont, California campus. I courted investors, bought equipment, and ran the club while attending school. The gym was an immediate hit, and twelve months later my P&L served as sweet vindication for my C-. Better still, an entrepreneur was born.

The fitness industry at the time — this would be in the late 70s — was dominated by weight machines and weightlifters, most of them men. Since my club was relatively small, I only had space for one locker room, so the male and female members were admitted on alternate days. Consequently, I couldn't help but notice how few women the gym attracted. Building conspicuous muscle wasn't much of a draw for them, and there was little aerobic exercise to speak of at the time.

Since it seemed foolish to ignore half the potential market, I started casting around for something that might appeal to women. I soon found what I was after in a San Diego gym. That's where I first saw the Life Cycle, a stationary bike with an electronic display that allowed the rider to follow his progress across hilly terrain as he pedaled his way through a twelve-minute exercise program. Or rather, as *she* pedaled *her* way through it; all of the Life Cycles in the place were occupied by female members.

With the same impetuousness that had gotten me into the health club business, I struck a deal to become the worldwide distributor of the Life Cycle. I'd soon bought a motor home, affectionately called "Slugo," and had set out across country to show the bike off to any gym rat who cared to see it. I drove from coast to coast, setting up in health club and fitness center parking lots to pitch my vision of the industry's coed future. I had a Life Cycle bolted to the floor of my mobile home, and I lured club owners and managers out to ride it every chance I got.

I was so confident I'd stumbled upon the future of fitness that I had several hundred Life Cycles ready for shipment in a California warehouse. My enthusiasm, however, proved doggedly uncontagious. Over the course of nine months, I sold a pathetic eleven bikes. By the time I returned to the West Coast, I found myself nearly a half million dollars in debt. Desperation took hold. I sifted through my meager options and settled on the one that made the most sense to me at the time. I needed people to love the bike like I did, so I started giving Life Cycles away.

From the scores of contacts I'd made on my cross-country trip, I selected fifty health club owners and sent each of them a bike. Not to their gyms but to their homes. I wanted this gift to be seen for what it was — a personal gesture made freely with no obligation attached. I hardly knew what, if anything, to expect in return, and I certainly had no idea I was tapping into a potent human force that has informed and shaped social interaction for centuries.

Even if inadvertently, I was unleashing the irresistible power of reciprocation. The fifty club owners, once they'd accepted something for nothing, could hardly hope to let the debt go unanswered. We were now joined in what anthropologists call a "web of obligation." My unexpected gift had to be repaid somehow. The hardwiring of the human psyche demanded it.

I've since grown to appreciate the profound gravitational pull of reciprocity, but at the time, I was merely hoping to stave off ruin and help generate enthusiasm for a product I believed in. The expense of putting fifty free Life Cycles into the hands of people who might buy and deploy fleets of them seemed modest relative to my investment in the four hundred bikes sitting unwanted in my warehouse. I was doing what I had to do as a businessman, and I remained blind to the social science of my gesture until well after the orders started coming in.

Today, I calculate that each of the fifty Life Cycles I gave away directly resulted in ten bikes sold. And those bikes in turn sold more bikes, which sold more bikes, which sold more bikes. The company I started with a lone product I believed in would eventually morph into Life Fitness, the largest manufacturer of exercise equipment in the world.

The lesson of those fifty bikes helped shape my fundamental philosophy as a businessman. That first generation Life Cycle was far from perfect, and even though we were repairing and replacing units at a staggering clip, I insisted on an unconditional guarantee. The expense and aggravation were high initially, but our company was working all along to improve the design and mend the frailties. I wanted to maintain the connections I'd cultivated and sustain the goodwill of my customers. Reciprocity again. I was just as ensnared in that web of obligation and integrity as they were.

This sort of open-handed, good-service ethic served me well in my career. As Life Fitness grew into a behemoth of the industry, my philosophy as CEO never wavered. A handshake was as good as a contract. Every piece of equipment we sold was guaranteed without condition. And if a customer wasn't happy, I wasn't happy. If those seem stunningly simple as business principles go, it's only because they are.

Flash forward to March of 2005. I'd been losing strength in my arms over the course of the previous eight months, and I'd begun to experience uncommon muscle twitches that finally prompted a visit to the Mayo Clinic in Arizona for a full examination. After three days of tests, a clinic neurologist delivered the diagnosis, and it was devastating. Amyotrophic Lateral Sclerosis. I have Lou Gehrig's disease. To make matters worse, the diagnosis was followed by the news that there is no effective treatment for ALS and that the root cause of the affliction remains a medical mystery. Instead of discussing therapeutic options, the neurologist advised me to get my affairs in order.

I went into a tailspin of despair and depression that lasted well into the summer. Once I'd regained my balance, I tried to find out all I could about my disease and was hardly encouraged by the modest breadth and vigor of ALS research. ALS is what's known as an orphan disease. Only five to seven thousand domestic cases are diagnosed annually, and there may be a mere 30,000 people in the country at any given time with some stage of ALS.

The low incidence of the disease in combination with its neurological complexity has resulted in scattered pockets of plodding academic research, but no robust and concerted push to identify the cause or causes of ALS and develop a drug therapy for treatment. It soon became clear to me that finding a cure for this disease was only an emergency for the people unfortunate enough to have been diagnosed with ALS.

I finally located an ALS research facility tuned to a suitable pitch of desperation. It's known today as The ALS Therapy Development Institute and was founded by the brother of an ALS patient. I have since become deeply involved in the workings of the Institute and serve as Chairman of the Board of Directors. Our goal is to treat ALS much like a big pharmaceutical company would treat a far more prevalent affliction. Together with the Muscular Dystrophy Association (MDA), we're mounting a wholesale assault on ALS, approaching the disease with no prior assumptions as to potential cause or possible drug therapies. Consequently, we stand prepared to try any and everything to vanquish this disease, but this endeavor promises to be enormously expensive.

A significant part of my role with the Institute in-volves raising money, with the help of MDA, to support ALS TDI's research efforts. So I have gone back into business, after a fashion — the business of fundraising. My colleagues in the fitness industry have responded heroically. If we succeed in finding a cure for ALS, the owners and operators of our nation's health clubs, and the companies that manufacture and supply their equipment, will have played an outsized part in the effort. Many of these contributors know me, or at least know of me and my place in their industry, so I approached them with a ready advantage.

But I've also enjoyed eager and considerable support from complete strangers in business. Their response has been both surprising and enlightening. When I was running Life Fitness, I thought of myself as a good corporate citizen. I gave to causes when I was asked to, which is to say I wrote checks to charities. I wasn't in the habit of volunteering my time, and I didn't necessarily keep up with where my money went, what it did, and who it did it for. I made the donations. I wrote them off. It was all just part of doing business.

Recently, though, I've stumbled across a new business paradigm — new to me anyway. Its hallmark is institutionalized compassion, a kind of corporate social conscience, a full embrace of the web of obligations and generosity that connects us all. A philosophical commitment, that is to say, to reciprocity. When I approach such companies for contributions to Augie's Quest, which funds the Therapy Development Institute, and explain the challenges of ALS for both researchers and patients, I often come away not just with money but with conscripts, people eager to invest their time and their energy to make my disease a thing of the past. One CEO met my show of pleasant surprise with a remark I'll long remember. "A company," he said, "can have a soul too."

So my ALS fundraising has had the collateral effect of prompting me to think about business and how it's conducted these days. It hasn't escaped my notice that the "soulful" companies I've come across are also highly profitable ventures. They're well and creatively run. They prize their customers and vendors — just as I did — and treat them accordingly. Their employees are happy, productive, and well cared for. They invest in their communities. They're environmentally minded. Profit at any cost is not their god. And their executive officers make a point of giving compensation a good name.

I've seen this new trend in business described as "sustainable capitalism," which is handy as far as it goes, but it doesn't fully capture what the CEO in me recognizes as a fresh and inventive marriage of conscientious creativity with profitability.

The more exposure I had to this new business model, the more interested I became in the day-to-day tone and operation of companies that embrace compassion and social responsibility as guiding principles. I grew hungry for details about the nuts and bolts of managing such enterprises, keen to quiz the entrepreneurs and CEOs on their philosophical underpinnings. Perversely enough, I was in a pretty good position to satisfy my curiosity. Leaving my CEO bona fides aside and my willingness to travel anywhere to conduct an interview, who's going to say no when a guy with ALS comes calling?

This book is my attempt to make the most of that access. In the past two years, I've had the pleasure of long, illuminating conversations with some of this nation's most creative business men and women. The memories are indelible — an afternoon in the Seattle office of Howard Schultz just a few months after his return to a troubled Starbucks — a far-ranging discussion in Detroit on the brand of home economics that prompted Mike Ilitch to found Little Caesars Pizza — a visit with storied homeless advocate Father Joe Carroll whose raw entrepreneurial zeal has made his San Diego "village" a model of dignified human reclamation — a high-octane chat with jewelry designer

Cookie Lee about the hundred-million dollar business she started in her spare bedroom — a session at my kitchen table with Safeway CEO Steve Burd who laid out his visionary plan to bring affordable, comprehensive health coverage not just to his quarter million employees, but to the nation at large.

In all, I conducted 30 interviews. The subjects were generous with their time and free with their counsel and opinions. Many remarked they'd never sat for quite this sort of interview before, chiefly because our conversations weren't so much about them as about you, my readers. These are all enormously accomplished people, and their achievements are well chronicled and easily accessed. For my part, I was less interested in what they'd done than what they would advise others to do.

Is there a best way for the budding entrepreneur to grapple with rejection and failure, to keep a healthy perspective on success? What skills, what temperament, what ethics are most welcome in the workplace? Where does creative, unorthodox thinking come from, and can it be learned? What are the most significant differences between business as it's taught and business as it's practiced? In what ways does a commitment to charity, to philanthropy, affect the fabric and tone of a company? How does reciprocity in the workplace intersect with profitability? What lessons can be drawn from business mistakes that successes will never teach? Does a company with a conscience enjoy a competitive advantage in the marketplace?

Questions such as these opened rich avenues of discussion along with countless unanticipated byways, and I soon found my sessions yielding colorful anecdotes and enough invaluable insights to fill a comprehensive business handbook. To an even greater extent, I have written this book as a simple and thoughtful guide for the business of life. The challenge for me lay in making the most efficient use of what I was hearing. The veins were so productive that I was feeling a little swamped until, one evening, I happened across the film version of David Mamet's *Glengarry Glen Ross* on TV.

The story is built upon the frictions and hardships of a real estate sales force in Chicago in the 1960s. Though we never see the property on offer, the free-floating anxiety and routine tirades among the salesmen suggest meager goods in a poor market. The relationships between the men run hot and profane. The atmosphere of the piece is Darwinian — eat or be eaten. If this company has a soul, it's coal black.

The film version differs from the Pulitzer Prize-winning stage play in one notable particular. Mamet added a scene — and a character — for the movie. The scene takes the form of a harangue visited upon the salesmen by an executive from the home office, from "Mitch and Murray uptown." He's played by Alec Baldwin in full sneer, and his motivational message is laced with scattershot humiliation. Baldwin's character distills his sales philosophy in an acronym: ABC — Always Be Closing. "The only thing that matters in this life," Baldwin tells the deflated salesmen, "is to get them to sign on the line that is dotted."

I was struck by the antiquity of it all. The only thing that matters? Always be closing? Baldwin's character made Gordon "Greed-Is-Good" Gekko from *Wall Street* seem relatively saintly. Compared to what I'd heard in my interviews, the thrust of Mitch and Murray's enterprise was little short of medieval. It might have been a fictional business, but the drive and the impulses were real enough in their day. For that era, for those principles, "Always be closing." could well have been a fitting prescription.

Not anymore. As a result of exhaustive conversations with the best and the brightest of the business world, coupled with my personal experience and evolving instincts, I've developed my own prescription for getting ahead in business without falling behind in life. Mine may not be as pithy as Mamet's, but it's sure to be more timely and more useful.

What follows are five lessons in sustainable success — for the entrepreneur, for the uneasy executive, for the young business neophyte, and for anyone who wants to live well by doing good. Please take as needed and apply liberally.

The Contributors

(in order of appearance)

Howard Schultz — He is the CEO of Starbucks and the driving force behind the coffee culture we know today. It was Schultz who discovered the latte in Austria and brought it stateside. His conviction that a business could be built upon made-to-order coffee drinks probably spared most of us a life of freeze-dried crystals. Schultz's company has long been known for its enlightened and compassionate treatment of employees, which is in keeping with Schultz's stated goal of making Starbucks "the sort of business I wished my father had worked for." From 2000 to 2008, Howard Schultz gave up his day-to-day responsibilities at Starbucks to devote his time and attention to his role as majority owner of the Seattle SuperSonics. Early 2008 saw his return to the executive suite to help guide the company he built through an ongoing turbulent passage. Standards at Starbucks had slipped over the years, in Schultz's view, and rebuilding the brand is sure to put Howard Schultz's elemental business philosophy to the test. "*Everything,*" he is fond of saying, "matters."

Glen Tullman — Tullman is the CEO of Allscripts, an electronic health records company with the mission of making illegible physician prescriptions a thing of the past. Prescription errors contribute to the deaths of 7,000 patients a year, which Glen often notes is the equivalent of one fully loaded Boeing 737 crashing each week for 12 months straight. No small thing. Glen is a social anthropologist by training and an accomplished amateur magician. He started his career in the White House Office of Management and Budget, serving in both the Carter and Reagan administrations. He eventually went into business with his older brother at Certified Collateral, which offered automated claims processing for the insurance industry. The medical appetite for eHealth services has skyrocketed in the last few years, and Tullman has positioned Allscripts on the cutting edge of the trend. In 2006 alone, the company saw its profits swell by 89%, and Glen was recently named Ernst and Young's Entrepreneur of the Year. Tullman's touch, however, isn't entirely golden. We spoke at some length about his involvement in Latenite Magic, a proposed chain of theme restaurants that Glen intended to build in partnership with magician David Copperfield. The inaugural venue in Times Square was abandoned near completion, and Glen's account of Latenite Magic's failure was one of the more fascinating bits of conversation I heard.

Scott Olivet — Scott is the CEO of Oakley, Inc., manufacturer of premium sunglasses and apparel. He was lured to Oakley from Nike, where Scott oversaw the acquisitions of Cole Haan, Converse, and Hurley. Before that, Olivet served as Senior Vice President for real estate, store design, and construction for The Gap, Inc. His responsibilities extended to Banana Republic and Old Navy venues as well. Scott has somehow married a flair for numbers and an impeccable gift for design in the same cranium, exceedingly rare in the executive suite. Our conversation was an exhaustive exploration of _authenticity_ as a business asset.

General Peter Pace — Most recently, General Pace was the Chairman of the Joint Chiefs of Staff and was the first Marine ever appointed to that post. He has also served as the Commanding Officer of the 2nd Battalion, First Marines, Deputy Commander of Marine Forces in Somalia, Commander of U.S. Marine Forces Atlantic/Europe/South, Commander in Chief of the United States Southern Command, and Vice-Chairman of the Joint Chiefs of Staff. Pace was elevated to Chairman of the Joint Chiefs in 2005, just over two years after the commencement of hostilities in Iraq. Pace's views were occasionally out of step with those of the Bush Administration and Secretary Rumsfeld, particularly on the issue of torture, where the General took the firm position that "it is the absolute responsibility of every U.S. service member, if they see inhumane treatment being conducted, to intervene to stop it." In June of 2008, new Secretary of Defense Robert Gates announced he would advise the President against renominating Pace as Chairman of the Joint Chiefs. Gates cited worries about contentious confirmation hearings. General Pace officially retired from the Marine Corps on October 1, 2007. He now serves as Chairman of the Board of Pelican Products, a manufacturer of protective equipment cases. Our conversation touched upon strains of tactical and strategic thinking as they apply to business, and we talked at some length of General Pace's experience in dealing with famously difficult personalities. I was interested in learning how a man trained in warfare succeeds in keeping the collegial peace.

Andrew Cherng — Andrew Cherng grew up in the restaurant business, primarily as a waiter. His father was a chef, but the two had only worked for hire before they joined forces to open the Panda Inn in Glendale, California in 1973. By chance, a family of shopping mall developers became regular, enthusiastic customers and suggested to the Cherngs that they bring their classic Chinese cuisine to shopping mall food courts throughout the country. The result is Panda Express. The chain now boasts more than one thousand restaurants spread across thirty-seven states. In 2007, The Panda Restaurant Group realized $1 billion in sales, and the company famously pays its 13,000 employees well in excess of minimum state and federal wages. During our conversation, Andrew Cherng repeatedly touched upon his passion for conservation and his commitment to environmental responsibility, not what I might have expected from the founder of a massive take-out food chain. But then, Andrew Cherng proved to be full of surprises.

Maria de Lourdes Sobrino — Sobrino is the founder, President, and CEO of Lulu's Dessert Factory of Anaheim, California. Better known by her nickname, Lulu Sobrino started her working life as a florist in Mexico City, but an economic downturn drove her north to California where, while employed as a programmer for IBM, she all but stumbled across a new business venture. When she was unable to find the gelatin desserts she'd enjoyed in Mexico, Lulu began making them for herself and her neighbors, who encouraged her to market them. She started small with consignment sales to first-generation Mexican grocers, and the response among their customers was immediate and enthusiastic. Today, Lulu's Desserts occupies a 64,000-square-foot factory that produces gelatins, parfaits, and puddings available worldwide. In our conversation, Lulu volunteered her three keys to success: responsibility, dedication, and hard, hard work.

Mike Gray — Mike started his business life in 1971 at St. John Knits, a women's clothier co-founded by Mike's parents From 1986 to 1991, Mike served as President of St. John, but he left the following year in order to "get out from under my father's shadow," he told me. In 1992, Mike invested in Sweet Life, a boutique bakery in Newport Beach, California, that he would help grow over the next 15 years into a specialty food services company with annual revenues of $100 million. Today, Sweet Life supplies its cookies and cinnamon buns (better known as Cinnamelts) to McDonald's and provides similar items to Four Seasons Hotels, Walt Disney Company, and Domino's Pizza. In 2007, Mike Gray engineered the sale of Sweet Life to Fresh Start Bakeries, which supplies hamburger buns and baked goods to McDonald's to the tune of a half billion dollars a year. Sweet Life's growth from a small retail bakery to a highly automated plant with 200 employees was halting and rocky. Mike laid out the process for me, which we dissected and discussed to better understand what went wrong and, ultimately, what went very right.

Wing Lam — The co-founder of Wahoo's Fish Taco, Wing Lam looks like a surfer because he is one. He's out on his board most mornings before he heads into work. Wing and his brothers, Ed and Mingo, came up with the idea for Wahoo's in 1988. They were already surfers at the time and had developed a taste for seaside taco-cart cuisine, which they hoped to recreate under a roof. They opened their first Wahoo's with the help of a $30,000 loan from their parents. Wing was largely in charge of the menu, a blend of Asian, Brazilian, and Mexican influences with an average check per customer in the vicinity of $8. The initial Southern California locations attracted surfers and skateboarders who loved the food and the vibe, and the manufacturers of their recreational equipment followed the talent. Most Wahoo's locations — and there are over fifty of them now as far east as Texas, as far west Honolulu — are heavily decorated with extreme sports equipment and manufacturers' stickers, all donated. "They came to us because their athletes ate in our restaurants," Wing commented. "They knew we were authentic." Today, Wahoo's Fish Taco is a $44 million enterprise, and the company has expanded without sacrificing its charm and appeal — its vibe. Wing and I discussed the elements of business authenticity in some depth along with Wing's ever-growing commitment to philanthropy as a cornerstone of his life in business and out of it.

Cookie Lee — Following a series of high-pressure marketing jobs with Mattel, Johnson & Johnson, and Revlon, Cookie Lee reconsidered her career path. Her parents had been hardworking Chinese immigrants, and Cookie (her given name is Debra Lin) grew up as a latch-key kid, tending to herself and her brother while her mother and father earned a living. She wanted something else for her own children, and was determined to shape a career that would strike a healthy balance between work and play. To that end, Cookie turned her eye for design and her talent for jewelry making into a growing business. Founded 16 years ago, Cookie Lee, Inc. — a party-plan jewelry company (think Mary Kay Cosmetics or Tupperware but for bling) — recently welcomed its one hundred thousandth sales consultant and boasts annual revenues approaching $150 million. Cookie Lee continues to design the entire line of jewelry and yet appears to sustain the executive/mother balance she was seeking when she gave over her corporate career. Our

16

conversation ended when the time came for Cookie to pick up her children at school.

Maureen Zehntner — In March of 2008, Maureen was officially named the CEO of the University of California Irvine Medical Center, where she'd been serving as interim CEO since 2005. As one University Chancellor put it, "After an exhaustive national search, we concluded the best candidate was already in our midst." She was not only the best candidate to run the hospital but very likely the most practically qualified as well, given Maureen's nursing background. "I went into my career because I care about what happens to patients," she explained. "I want every patient who visits our medical center to know they've received the highest quality care." Our conversation touched on the subtle (and sometimes not so subtle) biases against women in the executive suite. We spoke at length of Maureen's unusual progress from bedside patient care to the CEO's office, with a special emphasis on Maureen's relationship with the doctors and surgeons who make UC Irvine one of the premier care facilities in the western United States.

George Fisher — An engineer by training, Fisher holds a Ph.D. in applied mathematics from Brown University and began his career in research at Bell Laboratories. He joined Motorola, Inc. in 1976 where he rose through the ranks — Senior Vice President, Assistant General Manager of the Communications Sector, Deputy to the Chief Executive Officer — to become CEO in 1988 and Chairman of the Board from 1990 to 1993. In October of that year, George Fisher was named Chairman, President, and CEO of the Eastman Kodak Company, which was struggling to leave film behind and enter the digital age. Fisher left Kodak in January of 2000 and has since been deeply involved in international trade issues through his participation on the President's Advisory Council for Trade Policy and Negotiations. He also serves on the boards of AT&T, Eli Lilly, Delta Airlines, and General Motors. For a man with such a potent resume, George Fisher proved surprisingly modest and self-effacing in person. "I never wanted to be a CEO," he admitted. "I think I was a success in business because I was a failure in so many other things."

Kenneth E. Behring — Ken has lived the American dream, rising from Depression-era poverty in rural Wisconsin to join the Forbes 400 list of the richest Americans. But during the last decade, he has worked with even more diligence in giving back to the world and to people in need.

From his first career as an automobile dealer, he entered the world of real estate development and created numerous planned communities, including the city of Tamarac in Florida and the world-renowned Blackhawk development in northern California. He is a past owner of the Seattle Seahawks, has partnerships with hundreds of oil companies, and is now helping China develop a national model for senior living.

Subsequent to a personal epiphany about the joy of giving, Ken has made it his personal mission to help those in need. His donations of food, medical supplies, clothing, toys and educational materials have helped people in the most impoverished nations on earth. He doesn't just write checks... his boots are on the ground and he gets personally involved. On his 72nd birthday in 2000, he started the Wheelchair Foundation, which has delivered 800,000 wheelchairs to disabled people in 47 countries. "I once shook 500 hands of people who had just received new wheelchairs on a delivery trip," Ken recalled. "We don't share the same language but their huge smiles and bright eyes spoke to me."

Joining forces with the Lions Club, Ken provides cataract surgeries and eye care in developing countries. He has reinvigorated National History Day here in America, supports global efforts for clean water, and has gifted $100 million to the Smithsonian. He remains an active business entrepreneur, but charity work is his passion and purpose.

Father Joe Carroll — In 1982, Father Joe Carroll was appointed by San Diego's bishop to address the needs of the city's poor and homeless population. To that end, Father Joe assumed leadership of St. Vincent DePaul Village, a center-city charitable mission with a $600,000 annual operating budget. Under Father Joe's guidance, that budget has swelled to $35 million annually, and what's popularly known as Father Joe's Villages now offers an innovative and dignified hand up to San Diego's neediest population. A plain-spoken Bronx native, Father Joe has taken an entrepreneurial approach to addressing the thorny, underlying causes of poverty and homelessness. The result is a comprehensive program with an emphasis on education, health care, job training, and personal responsibility. Father Joe's San Diego campus features a high school, a medical clinic, dormitories for the "residents," and a first-class culinary program that is now supplying cooks and chefs to restaurants throughout the area. "Private industry could learn from us," Father Joe articulated. "We never give up on an employee. We let them think big. We give them a chance to grow." Father Joe's model for helping the homeless back into society is taking hold throughout the country in cities like Austin and New

Orleans. When I asked for one of his favorite success stories, Father Joe told me about a 75-year-old resident who had learned to read in one of the campus classrooms. "Now you never see him without a book," Father Joe said. "Imagine the world that's opened up to him."

Paul Jacobs — The CEO of Qualcomm (short for Quality Communications) is an electrical engineer by training and currently holds more than two dozen patents in the field of wireless technology. The company was co-founded by Paul's father, Irwin Jacobs, in 1985. Four short years later, Qualcomm rolled out Code Division Multiple Access (CDMA), a communications protocol that is the foundation of wireless telephony as we know it today. The technology is based on the idea that multiple frequencies can be used to send a single radio signal. This innovation of "frequency hopping" is credited to Hollywood screen siren Hedy Lamarr (I'm not kidding!) and was perfected and implemented by Qualcomm. Today, the company holds over 7,000 wireless technology patents, which it licenses to cell phone manufacturers worldwide. Under Paul Jacobs' guidance, Qualcomm has become a model of horizontal integration in its field, encouraging and materially supporting technological development across the breadth of the wireless arena. Qualcomm is also widely known for its philanthropic pursuits, and Jacobs has labored tirelessly to sustain the company's commitment to the betterment of the communities in which its employees live and work.

Mike Ilitch — As a young man, Mike Ilitch played minor league baseball with dreams of taking the field as a Detroit Tiger. He supported himself in the off season by making and selling pizzas in a Detroit nightclub. When a knee injury ended Ilitch's baseball career, Mike and his wife, Marian, opened a pizzeria in the suburb of Garden City. The place was known as Little Caesars Pizza Treat and served as ground zero for what would become a restaurant empire. A commitment to value — two pizzas for the price of one — and a memorable catchphrase — Pizza!Pizza! — helped fuel a franchise expansion that led to 5,000 Little Caesars worldwide by the early 1990s. A former Marine, Mike Ilitch has recently instituted a generous program to provide career opportunities for wounded soldiers returning from Iraq in the form of free Little Caesars franchises. He is also the owner of the Detroit Tigers and the Detroit Red Wings, which Ilitch plainly considers more of a hobby and indulgence than a business. "Owning sports teams," he confided with me in his conference room overlooking Comerica Park, "is a great way to lose money."

Ray Thurston — Ray began his career as a bicycle courier for his father's delivery company and went on to found SonicAir in 1976, which specialized in the rapid, same-day delivery of perishable medical supplies and exotic diagnostic equipment from coast to coast. Under Thurston's direction, SonicAir became the model of supply-chain efficiency, and in 1995, the company was bought by UPS in a bid to better compete with FedEx for its overnight clients. Thurston stayed on as CEO, retiring in 1998 after doubling the revenue of the UPS Logistics Group. Since then, Ray has shared his talent for wringing efficiency out of business structures and practices as a consultant, and he has taken a special interest in helping to engineer a cure for breast cancer. Most recently, Ray has developed a working relationship with the Translational Genomic Research Institute (TGen) as both a substantial donor and a supply-chain management expert. TGen's mission is to translate genomic discoveries into practical advances in human health, and Ray's goal is to help them accomplish that mission with all deliberate speed.

George Argyros — George Argyros is probably distinct among billionaires in having embarked upon his business career as a grocery store bag boy. He worked his way up to store manager at the ripe age of 21 and, in casting around for additional opportunities, fairly fell into real estate. Young Argyros took advantage of the interstate boom in Southern California in the 1950s to buy up parcels around highway exchanges that he sold to oil companies for service station lots. He then graduated to property management, most of it commercial and apartment space. From 1981 to 1989, Argyros owned the Seattle Mariners baseball team. He was appointed in 1990 to the board of the Federal Home Loan Mortgage Corporation (Freddie Mac) by then President George H. W. Bush, and he was selected by the younger Bush to serve as our ambassador to Spain in 2001. It was in this capacity that George Argyros represented our nation at the time of the Madrid bombings on the 11th of March, 2004. Though our conversation was wide-ranging, Argyros returned time and again to integrity as a key to success in all things. "Always be honest," he advised me. "There's a lot less to remember that way."

Robert Day — Day is founder, chairman, and CEO of the Trust Company of the West Group, Inc., an L.A.-based investment firm with $160 billion under management. He also serves as President and Chief Executive Officer of the W. M. Keck Foundation, one of this nation's most generous philanthropic organizations with an emphasis on scientific, engineering, and medical research in the United States. The organization may be best known by the general public for its longstanding support of PBS's *Sesame Street* on KCET in Southern California. The Keck Foundation was the creation of William Myron Keck, Robert Day's grandfather and the founder of the Superior Oil Company. A couple of interesting Robert Day facts: he deplores email, insists on reading the physical copies of four newspapers a day, and is an Argentinean paddle ball enthusiast.

Dean Rasmussen — In 1964, Dean Rasmussen's father, Carl, started C.A. Rasmussen, Inc. in Lancaster, California with a couple of motor graders and a skeleton staff. A few years later, his eldest son, Dean, joined him after a stint in the Merchant Marine and the pursuit of an engineering degree at Arizona State University. Dean's two brothers soon signed on as well, and the quartet of Rasmussens built the company on highway and housing construction. During the 1990s, Rasmussen equipment could be found on jobs from the northern California border clear to San Diego. Dean has since retired from the company his father started, and a third generation of Rasmussens has taken the rudder. Dean had much to say on management — both business and family — and the lessons he drew from his Merchant Marine service that stayed with him throughout his business career.

Patrick Fuscoe — The founder and namesake of Fuscoe Engineering, Pat specializes in environmentally responsible development and currently serves as Chairman of the Board of Miocean, a non-profit organization dedicated to reducing urban runoff and protecting the integrity of Southern California's beaches. "I believe we're all connected in the web of life," Pat explained, "and everything we do affects each strand of the web." Pat has long provided pro bono services for Habitat for Humanity, HomeAid, and the Boy Scouts. He is an annual sponsor of the Ocean Institute's Adopt-A-Class program, which funds educational trips for underprivileged children. Pat and I engaged in a lengthy discussion of activism in business practices, particularly where they meet with profitability. Pat's firm practices what it preaches in terms of environmental responsibility, and Pat's view of his role as an environmentally sensitive engineer and developer has significantly affected who he works with and who he works for — but not in the ways you might imagine.

Peter Ueberroth — In 1962, Ueberroth founded the First Travel Corporation which, upon its sale in 1980, was the second largest travel business in North America with 300 retail agencies nationwide. He was lead organizer of the 1984 Summer Olympics in Los Angeles, which earned Ueberroth Man-of-the-Year honors from both *Time Magazine* and *The Sporting News.* Ueberroth served as Commissioner of Major League Baseball from 1984 to 1989 and was the leader of the Rebuild Los Angeles project following the 1992 Rodney King riots. In partnership with Arnold Palmer and Clint Eastwood, Ueberroth engineered the purchase of the Pebble Beach Corporation in 1999 and thereby returned one of this country's premier golf courses to American ownership. He has been a Director of The Coca-Cola Company since 1986 and Chairman of The Contrarian Group (a management and investment firm) since 1989. He also served as Chairman of the Board of Directors of the current U.S. Olympic Committee. How he found a couple of leisurely hours to spend with me, I'll never know.

Steve Burd — Steve Burd has been the President and CEO of Safeway, Inc. for a remarkable 16 years. The grocery store chain is the third largest in North America with over 1,700 stores and nearly a quarter million employees. Under Burd's guidance, Safeway has become a staggeringly impressive fundraising machine with checkers soliciting customers for donations to specific causes, depending on the calendar. Safeway's vendors are also deeply involved in the philanthropy, and the impulse springs from Burd and his colleague's belief that a company that fails to help improve the communities it serves — where its employees live — won't succeed and thrive. Steve Burd takes much the same view of Safeway's 250,000 employees and has devoted much of his recent time and energy to improving their health and happiness through a revolutionary approach to medical care. In the calendar year of 2006, Safeway paid $1 billion in health care costs. Burd has since spearheaded an effort that rewards healthy living — much like auto insurance companies reward safe driving — and introduced the sorts of sensible efficiencies into diagnosis and early detection that save both lives and money.

Edmund Shea — With his brother Peter and his cousin John, Edmund Shea serves as an integral part of the J.F. Shea Company's fourth generation of family management. Originally a plumbing supply wholesaler out of Portland, Oregon, the J.F. Shea Company entered the field of heavy construction in the early 1900s and has either managed or participated in a number of celebrated American engineering projects. The J.F. Shea Company built the foundation piers for the Golden Gate Bridge in San Francisco and served as construction manager for the Hoover Dam. At present, the J.F. Shea Company is lead contractor on the $4 billion

Second Avenue subway line in Manhattan. Under the guidance of Edmund, Peter, and John Shea, the company has expanded into residential development and construction with Shea Homes. Edmund Shea was also one of the earliest and most successful venture capitalists in Silicon Valley, participating in relationships with Compaq Computer, Altera Corporation, America West Airlines, and Novell, among others. Edmund and his relatives would be celebrated for their far-ranging philanthropy if their native modesty didn't conceal much of it from public view.

Jeff Moorad — Jeff currently serves as general partner and CEO of the San Diego Padres of the National League's western division, and he readily admits his route to team management wasn't the least bit conventional. "I came from the dark side," Jeff told me. In 1983, Jeff founded Moorad Sports Management, which would become a potent force in player representation. Initially, Jeff's focus was on Major League Baseball, but after combining forces with Leigh Steinberg in 1985, the firm expanded to represent a celebrated roster of NFL players as well, including 49ers quarterback Steve Young and Cowboys quarterback Troy Aikman. During their eighteen-year partnership, Moorad and Steinberg negotiated more than $3 billion in athletic contracts. Before Jeff, no players' agent had ever moved to the management side of the equation, and though there was widespread skepticism about Moorad at the time, his experience as a player's rep has served him well in the Diamondbacks executive suite. "I'd already done business with the league's thirty teams," Jeff said, "so I was in a good position to pick and choose among many of the best practices that I'd observed over the years. That's been a real advantage for me in shifting to this side of the table."

George Gorton — If the name sounds familiar, you might have come across it in Woodward and Bernstein's _All The President's Men_. In 1972, young George Gorton worked for the Committee to Re-Elect the President, better known as CREEP. He served as the Nixon campaign's national college director and was pilloried for having paid a George Washington University student to spy on antiwar activists. Gorton was singled out in a _Washington Post_ editorial as a corruptor of America's youth. He was only twenty-three years old at the time. His stint in the political wilderness proved short-lived. George Gorton served as Jack Ford's press secretary beginning in 1976 and went on to work on the presidential campaign of a Panamanian puppet candidate under the direction of General Manuel Noriega. In 1994, Gorton managed Governor Pete Wilson's successful campaign for re-election, which hinged on Wilson's support for anti-immigration Proposition 187, and Gorton worked surreptitiously in Russia in 1996 to help re-elect Boris Yeltsin. His part in a movie based on those events, _Spinning Boris_, was played by Jeff Goldblum. More recently, Gorton served as the lead consultant on Arnold Schwarzenegger's successful gubernatorial bid and has founded an online university for political consultants. In person, Gorton proved a curious blend of hard-nosed politics and eastern spirituality. Refreshingly un-ideological, Gorton was incisive about people and persuasion, not just in politics but in business as well.

Alan Schwartz — Alan Schwartz was taught tennis by his father when he was just a boy. He competed throughout his school, captained the Yale tennis team, and went on to win eight national championships in every age bracket from 65 years old until a fused ankle took him out of compe play. Today, Alan counts tennis as far more than a recreational force in his life. It has been at the center of his business pursuits as well. In 1969, Alan co-founded the Midtown Tennis Club in Chicago with his father, Kevie. It was the first purpose-built indoor tennis facility in the country and served as the foundation for what would become 13 sports resorts nationwide, now known as Midtown Athletic Clubs. Alan helped write and teach the first management training course for sports club professionals, which today is commonly available at the university level. He created the first industry-wide program for workers' compensation insurance, co-created a patented three-week tennis teaching program — Tennis in No Time — and served as President of the United States Tennis Association from 2003 through 2004. Schwartz is widely known by his peers for having brought business professionalism and high ethical standards to the health club industry at a time when it was practicing neither. Alan credits tennis as a guiding force in his life, not just athletically but morally as well. "When you play fair and play hard, you learn how to win and how to lose," he reflected.

S. Paul Musco — In 1981, Paul Musco founded Gemini Industries, an Orange County based company that pioneered the process of extracting platinum and palladium from spent automobile catalytic convertors. Gemini is now the largest operation of its sort in the world, and as the prices of heavy metals have soared, so have Paul Musco's fortunes. Now in his 80s, Musco devotes the bulk of his energy to a wide range of philanthropic pursuits, including but not confined to the L.A. Opera, Opera Pacific, the Muscular Dystrophy Association, and Chapman University, where Paul Musco and his wife have established a Chair in Italian. One of ten children, Paul Musco was born in Rhode Island to Sicilian immigrants. He was trained as a pharmacist in the Navy, which he joined as a sixteen-year-old. His career has carried him through a range of employment and a full array of workplace experiences that have informed the generous and open-handed operation of Gemini Industries. Paul Musco's insights into the best working atmosphere of a thriving business and how to create it were fascinating.

John Ondrasik — You may know John as the lead singer and songwriter for the band _Five For Fighting_. I met him when I hired John to entertain at an ALS fundraiser. He performed winningly to a raucous crowd and then donated his entire (and sizable) fee to the cause of ALS research. John's family is Slovak on his father's side, and John's grandfather started and built a wire business in Los Angeles where John worked — making shopping carts — while he was trying to find his way in the music world. A song he considers tossed off, _Superman (It's Not Easy)_, turned into a substantial hit for John and his band. He would be invited to sit alone at the piano and play _Superman_ at the post 9/11 concert for New York in Madison Square Garden. "I saw these big burly firemen crying while I sang," John recalled. "That might be the most important thing I'll ever do." John's take on creativity and artistic self-employment — the costs and the considerable benefits — opened a window into a side of business life that few of the other contributors were equipped to address.

Jeffrey Trent — Jeffrey is the President and Scientific Director of TGen. I spoke to Dr. Trent in conjunction with my conversation with Ray Thurston, who has recently brought his talent for logistics and business efficiency to the operation of TGen. Trent (a research scientist by training and current head of TGen's Melanoma Therapeutics Lab) and Thurston may come from two different worlds where business practices are concerned, but they've joined together in an attempt to radically accelerate the speed of medical discovery and therapy development. Theirs is a classic case of taking what's best in one discipline and attempting to apply it to another. If they succeed — and there are signs that they just might — the stodgy pace of medical research (not to mention the course of humanity) will be changed forever in the process.

Lesson One:

Always Be Curious

In 1981, Howard Schultz was working for the Swedish housewares company Hammarplast. He served as U.S. operations manager based in New York, and he noticed a Seattle retailer was placing uncommonly large orders for one of his company's drip coffee makers. The customer was Starbucks Coffee, Tea, and Spice, and Schultz was surprised to discover that, with only four stores, Starbucks was outstripping Macy's in sales of this particular item. Schultz announced to his wife, "I want to know what's going on out there." He bought a ticket to Seattle and changed the history of caffeine.

This is precisely the brand of curiosity worth nurturing and encouraging. It is vital, nagging, deeply inquisitive and, most significantly, *active*. We've all wondered about all manner of things idly and in passing, but how many of us have bought that figurative ticket to Seattle to find out what we need to know? If my conversations over the past year with entrepreneurs and CEOs have been marked by a reliably recurring theme it is this: hunger matters. Not just a hunger to succeed but a hunger to know. What works and why? What doesn't and why not? How best is success created and duplicated and how might failure be avoided? And this doesn't apply only to large, strategic considerations but to daily tactical issues as well.

The workable answers are rarely at hand. They need to be tracked down and dug up. Thriving businesses aren't congenial to mere head scratching and intellectual lethargy. There's no need for it. No time for it. Hunger matters most, which is why executive suites around the world are heavily populated with connoisseurs of active curiosity.

On the business evolutionary scale, the entrepreneur is probably the most inquiring specimen since entrepreneurial pursuits are often driven by a combination of practical observation and informed intuition. It's not unusual for intellectual hunger in the entrepreneur to run at a fever pitch. He or she is constantly scouring for solutions to business problems and fresh approaches to market needs. The entrepreneur's curiosity is little short of forensic. They want to know how everything works and why — and how everything might work better.

"That's fundamentally a destructive process," Glen Tullman told me, and he should know. Tullman is the quintessential entrepreneur. He helped create, refine, and sell several businesses. Glen serves currently as the CEO of Allscripts, a company on the cutting edge of the behemoth healthcare/medical services industry. When Glen arrived, Allscripts functioned primarily as a pill repackager for doctors. Under his direction, the company has developed and deployed software that drains virtually all of the human error from the prescription filling process.

Doctors have been writing scripts much the same way for a generation or two. This was a practice that seemed to work. Tullman, however, chose to train his interest and focus his curiosity on the failure rate, a gaudy 7,000 prescription-related deaths a year due to miscommunication between doctors and pharmacists. When compared to the total number of prescriptions filled in this nation annually (3.4 billion in 2005), 7,000 mistakes is statistically insignificant. But once a human life is attached to each error, the mistakes become something else altogether.

Tullman, through Allscripts, performed the entrepreneur's essential service of bringing his curiosity to bear on a "sound" process in order to locate its frailties. "Entrepreneurs," Tullman confessed, "are a pain in the ass. They want to break things that appear to be working fine. A good manager takes what is and tries to make it work as well as possible. An entrepreneur looks at things as they are and tries to make them better." Tullman was quick to allow that "every entrepreneur makes a lot of mistakes, but they work fast enough to recover quickly. In many cases, they don't even remember their mistakes, or they call them *"smart experiments."* Glen laughed. "Wrong. A smart experiment would have worked."

In the late 1970s, when I was struggling to market the Life Cycle, I made a point of applying my entrepreneurial curiosity to various thriving businesses. If somebody had made good in their field, I wanted to know how and why, particularly where it came to unconditional guarantees. One of the companies I studied was Domino's Pizza.

At the time, Domino's had just started guaranteeing delivery in thirty minutes or the pizza was free. Domino's had held focus groups of customers to determine what was most important to them — lowest price, best tasting pizza, or hot pizza in thirty minutes. Armed with the knowledge that, as far as their customers were concerned, hot pizza delivered fast mattered most, Domino's organized its entire business around velocity since they were freed from having to make the best pizza in any market or the cheapest one.

The promise of *hot pizza fast* dictated the number of ovens in each store, the number of drivers at each location, and what zip codes each franchise could afford to take orders from. Failure was easily measured in the number of pizzas given away.

I took a lesson from Domino's experience and tried to apply a similar metric to my business at Life Fitness. We held focus groups, and customers told us they wanted a repairman to fix a broken machine within forty-eight hours. By way of response, we began hiring repairmen and women strategically located around the country who we could deliver on short notice against our unconditional guarantee. The repair was important, but the timing of it was clearly more important. If I hadn't been willing to look outside my own experience and my own business, if I hadn't exercised my entrepreneurial curiosity, I might well have learned the same lesson but only eventually and at some cost. Better to pursue one of Glen Tullman's "smart experiments" than no experiment at all.

But the sort of entrepreneurial appetite Tullman described isn't just for entrepreneurs. Improving practices and processes in the workplace is every interested employee's job. So the question becomes — if you're not the boss — are you an interested employee? "At The Gap," Scott Olivet described, "I managed 1,000 people who had wildly different motivations for going to work every day. I thought my job would be 80% strategic renovation and 20% people, but it turned out to be exactly the reverse." Olivet's career has taken him from The Gap, to Nike, and now to the top spot at Oakley. He's rubbed elbows with all sorts of colleagues along the way, and he makes a ready distinction between those people just showing up for a paycheck and the employees fully invested in their careers.

"Other than brief periods and bad days," Scott insisted, "I don't feel like I'm going to a job." That might be a readier sentiment from a CEO than from the guy changing the toner cartridge, but if the not-just-a-job attitude is embraced early on and sustained throughout a career, the chances of success are sure to be improved. General Peter Pace expressed much the same idea in a slightly different fashion. "Grow where you're planted," he summarized.

Peter Pace's forty-four-year career is proof of the wisdom of that advice. Pace, planted in the Marine Corps early on, led a rifle squad in Hue City during the Tet Offensive of 1968. He rose steadily through the ranks and assumed the command of the 2nd Batallion, First Marines before serving as Deputy Commander of Marine Forces in Somalia in 1993, the year of the battle of Mogadishu and *Black Hawk Down*. General Pace was named Commander of the U.S. Southern Command in 2000 and assumed the Vice-Chairmanship of the Joint Chiefs of Staff in 2001. Upon the retirement of General Richard Meyers in 2005, Pace was selected by President George W. Bush for the chairmanship and was the first Marine to ever serve in that capacity. In the fall of 2007, Peter Pace retired from his beloved Marine Corps. He continues to serve on the President's Intelligence Board and the Secretary of Defense's Policy Board.

You might think a business career and a military career would have little in common, but General Pace assured me that a number of my assumptions about life in the Marine Corps specifically and the armed forces generally were, to be polite, inoperative.

"For folks who've not served in the military, it comes as a surprise that questioning orders, challenging your leaders, is thought good and healthy," General Pace observed. "I want to be sitting around a table with a lot of people. I want to be talking and thinking out loud. I encourage my people to push back and ask questions. A good soldier, after all, is somebody who is willing to take orders, give orders, understand that he should question the orders he gets and that people below him should question the orders he gives in a way that ensures the mission gets done with the most efficiency and effectiveness." So even with its emphasis on chain of command, the military — General Pace assured me — fully embraces the twin virtues of curiosity and questioning as keys to mission success.

Of course, there are various ways to get at information, some better than others. "I've learned to ask questions in such a way that invites an education," the General said. "'If you hadn't said that, I would have thought this. Can you educate me on why that's not right?' Now you've put your thought on the table without directly challenging the authority of the person you're questioning. They might take ownership of your idea or they might educate you. It always pays to remember, no matter how senior you are, you only know what you know. You don't know everything."

So in the military, just as in business, hunger matters on a fundamental level. And for very practical reasons. "The thing for which you're the least prepared will be the thing most likely to happen to you," General Pace assured me. "You need a broad enough background to adjust to what you know. I never conducted a war game that focused on Afghanistan or Iraq, but that's where we ended up. Fortunately, the skill sets were transferable. Working hard in

training gives you the ability to be mentally flexi\
the surprise comes." And the surprise, the General \
always comes.

So the safe assumption is that there's no end of learning. There's always something you don't know, probably
plenty you don't know, and the key is to *want* to know it.

Andrew Cherng, the co-founder of Panda Express,
raised the quintessential complementary business question:
"How do we get people to say 'There's a lot I don't know?'"
Still privately held, Panda Express boasts over 13,000
employees at nearly 1,200 locations. Revenues have recently
topped $1 billion annually, so Andrew Cherng has a
conspicuous talent for and an ongoing interest in doing the
right thing the right way. If our conversation was any
indication, Andrew spends a fair amount of time both
visiting his restaurants, no matter how far-flung, and
thinking about his employees.

"The ideal Panda Express employee," Andrew out-
lined, "is the person who is willing to change, willing to
work on himself and take on responsibility. Some people
choose to work on the task — get this done today, that done
tomorrow, etc. The question I want to ask people is, 'Who
are you helping?' Coming to work to get the job done, that's
the minimum. Most people are too task oriented. They don't
know about life, and they need to."

Lulu Sobrino of Lulu's Desserts echoed Andrew's
sentiments. "I want creative employees," she explained. "I
need people who motivate me, too. I look for initiative." And
Lulu made clear that initiative for her was closely linked to
hunger, to curiosity, to a thirst for knowledge, for
information. "Information," she said, "helps you be
realistic." Mike Gray, former CEO of Sweet Life, boiled the

matter down for me in the form of a question. "It's pretty simple," he said. "Are you going to be a brick or a sponge?"

Mike's parents founded St. John Knits. Initially, Mike's mother designed the fashions for the company and Mike's father marketed them. Today, St. John boasts four thousand employees and expects revenues in 2010 to top $400 million. Mike joined the family business in 1971 and served as President of the company from 1986 through 1991. In a bid to prove himself away from family ties, Mike struck out on his own in 1992 and purchased Sweet Life, a southern California retail bakery. While Mike planned all along to grow the company into something resembling the specialty food service dynamo it is today, the initial progress was halting and deeply frustrating for him.

"At Sweet Life," Mike told me, "we went for three years where I dumped a bunch of money in, and the business wasn't successful. I told everybody I would put money in one more time, and if it didn't work, that was it." Everything changed after that. "There was a paradigm shift in the way we did business from that moment on," Mike said. "We were profitable every quarter after that. Sometimes it's a curse to have plenty of money. We were wasting it. We were more prey than predator."

Mike's resolve to sink or swim changed the tone at Sweet Life and altered the company's approach to how they did business and who they hired. "After I decided to stop putting money in the business," Mike remembered, "we started hiring a different type of employee. We were drawn to people driven to succeed rather than just looking for a job. The hungry people came through the door. They always had, but now the culture had changed, and we were attracted to those sorts of people where we hadn't been before. If your business is going to succeed," he added, "your people have to stay hungry and stay focused. If you don't have the money to waste, it's easier to make sure they do that."

Mike then revealed a bit of a courtship story that didn't have to turn out nearly as well as it did. "My wife started at Sweet Life about ten years ago," he said, "and we didn't get along very well. She was a hunter rather than a farmer. She'd do whatever it took to get the kill, and the kill is selling. A farmer cultivates the business. We were driving down the road," Mike told me, "not married at the time, and she was giving me so much trouble that I pulled over and told her to get out of the car. I came back twenty minutes later to see if she was ready to start listening. Back at the office, I gave her a brick with a sponge glued to the top of it, and I asked her which she was going to be — the brick or the sponge."

Sponges grow where they're planted. Bricks lie fallow. The symbolism fits nearly every category of business endeavor, and I've rarely, if ever, strayed across a brick in a leadership position of a thriving business. People routinely advance in their careers thanks to hard work and open minds. A willingness to soak in information — an eagerness to learn — is never a liability, and no one I spoke with failed to bring up the fundamental educational value of labor. More often than not, business success is earned rather than received, and every job along the way is an occasion for instruction.

When Wing Lam and his brothers opened their first Wahoo's Fish Taco restaurant in 1988, they were effectively returning to the family business. For years, Wing's parents had owned and operated a popular Chinese restaurant on Orange County's Balboa Island, and Wing had worked his way through the business holding every possible job, no matter how menial. He approached each with the same spirit. "I was a good employee," Wing told me. "It didn't matter what I was doing. I always tried to leave a job better than I found it. When I was a dishwasher, I was the best dishwasher. When I was a delivery guy, I was the best delivery guy."

It may seem like a small thing, but the willingness to bring enthusiasm and conscientiousness to even the most unglamorous job is, at the core, entrepreneurial. When I visited with Howard Schultz, he touched upon the grand, overarching tone of the entrepreneurial spirit. "There was something creative inside me," he said. "I knew I wanted to paint my own canvas." Jewelry designer Cookie Lee put the same impulse in more practical terms. "I'm entrepreneurial," she recounted, "which means I empty the trash."

Ken Behring recalls his first unglamorous job and scraping out the inside of a used chicken coop he had purchased from a friend for $10. The coop served as his sales office for a startup used car business. "Customers never took too much time to make a decision," Ken joked, "because the smell of that chicken coop made them want to leave in a hurry."

He had leased a sunken lot on the outskirts of his Wisconsin hometown. But he was innovative and talked construction companies into paying him a few dollars to haul away fill dirt, which he used to level the lot for trade-in cars. He strung lights from poles around the lot, painted the coop and opened for business. "That first winter came on quicker than I thought," Ken admitted, "and I had no idea what the rain and snow would do to the ground I had built under the cars. Things began to sink and the light poles were bowing inward."

When he told me about the worst night of his life, even I was squirming. It was pitch dark with brutally cold temperatures, and his knuckles bled from working alone to "winterize" the cars with alcohol so the engine blocks wouldn't freeze. "It was awful work, lying in the mud underneath each car. I had to open the drain and rusted fluid poured down my freezing arms. It took me the entire day and night," Ken said, "but everything I had in the world was sitting on that lot and if it froze, it was all gone. I was never so miserable but I had to do it because there was just me."

Emptying the trash, winterizing cars on a sinking lot, intent on being the best dishwasher, the best delivery guy, the best any and everything — that's the entrepreneur in a nutshell. Today's business leaders were yesterday's curious hirelings. "I started out at a small startup company," Glen Tullman recalled, "a heat pump company. I was fascinated by the fact that in a small business, you had to do everything. I liked that." Maureen Zehtner, the CEO of the University of California's premier medical facility in Irvine, began in hospital work as a nurse. She insists she wouldn't be half the executive she is today but for her background. "I got my start at the bedside, emptying bedpans," she proudly admitted. "I think I got where I am by always trying to make things better — better for the patients, better for the doctors and the nurses. I never went into it looking to be a CEO. I just got aggravated."

"I'm a great believer in just-in-time education," George Fisher informed me. The former CEO of both Motorola and Kodak added, "When I need it, I get it." The ability to recognize personal deficiencies and rectify them, to make something constructive out of aggravation, to invite new experiences, to expand capabilities — these are the ways in which business success is created. Intellectual flexibility matters. To put it in Peter Pace's words, "you only know what you know," which leaves the world teeming with what General Pace's former boss, Donald Rumsfeld, famously referred to as "known unknowns." The trick is to make the latter the former in any way you can. It all begins with the right disposition.

"Sometimes people will come in with a resume," Glen Tullman told me, "and say 'I have ten years of experience,' but I'll look at it and tell them, 'No, you have one year of experience repeated ten times.' That's not a good thing."

Father Joe Carroll's homeless "campus" in San Diego, locally known as Father Joe's Villages, houses, feeds, educates, and trains around 900 residents at any given time. In effect, Father Joe is an employer in the business of training employees. His emphasis is on teaching the homeless of San Diego the skills to land a job while reinforcing the habits required to hold one. As a result, Father Joe has become wise in the ways of business from both sides of the equation. And it is an equation which, every now and then, will simply refuse to add up.

"I worked for the Post Office for a while," Father Joe recalled, "and if you ever want to see a company that kills ambition, that's it. At the Post Office, a new idea is like a disease." In that case, no amount of hunger, no degree of curiosity and flexibility would matter. What Father Joe learned from his time at the Post Office was that he didn't want to train people (or need to train people) to work at places like the Post Office.

At Life Fitness, I always encouraged new ideas because we needed them. When we started out, the fitness industry was young and evolving. Our first models of the Life Cycle operated on vacuum tubes. LED and solid state technology were just emerging, so we had all sorts of mechanical and technical problems that are difficult to even imagine today. When we started manufacturing treadmills, we had a hard time finding a practical way to shut the units down when users stepped off of them. As a result, we had an injury and liability problem when gym members tried, unwittingly, to mount active machines.

Our engineers were busy trying to develop a fix when I happened to discover one in the men's room. The new toilets in our building flushed automatically through the use of a brand new technology — infrared sensors. In a moment of water-closet inspiration, I realized a treadmill could be switched off the same way. We removed a sensor from one of our toilets and fixed it to a treadmill. It worked beautifully, and we suddenly had a fresh advantage to use against our competitors. The lesson for me was to keep my eyes and my mind open, no matter where I might be, since I could never know where the good ideas might be lurking.

Father Joe Carroll works to build that same sense of limitless possibility into his program in San Diego. "We try to teach our residents what it's like to live in the real world," Father Joe said. "We want our people to have the confidence to learn something new. If you're not teachable, in my view, you're not going anywhere." Father Joe is nothing if not consistent. He applies the identical approach to his staff. He insists his employees always be learning, testing, pushing, thinking. Initiative matters most to Father Joe. "My philosophy is simple," he observed. "If I have to get involved in your end of the operation, then I've hired the wrong person."

A short drive up Interstate 5 from Father's Joe's downtown San Diego campus lies another campus in what seems, cosmetically anyway, a different world. Qualcomm's La Jolla home office complex occupies a cluster of meticulously manicured high-rise buildings overlooking the rolling hills of this staggeringly affluent San Diego suburb. On the afternoon I arrived to interview Paul Jacobs, Qualcomm's CEO, several dozen employees were tidying up following a picnic on the grounds. I was struck by the range of nationalities on display — the United Nations quality of what proved to be a representative sample of Qualcomm's workforce. The company attracts the best candidates from all corners of the earth.

The Qualcomm executive suite is located in what can only be called an aerie — a spacious perch crowning the main office building that offers sweeping views of the scrubby Southern California hillsides, the network of intersecting highways, and the blue Pacific. Paul Jacobs met me in his elegantly understated conference room. He is tall, fit, forty-five years old, modest about his accomplishments, and frank about his missteps. Since I'd spent a large chunk of the previous afternoon with Father Joe Carroll, I couldn't help but compare the two in my head. The differences, I soon recognized, were all superficial.

Jacobs, an electrical engineer by training, is an easygoing Southern Californian to the bone. Father Joe is a bluff, blunt native of the Bronx who not only spends his days among San Diego's homeless population but his nights as well. He lives in a small, modestly furnished house opposite the main residence hall. But surface differences in appearance and circumstance between Jacobs and Father Joe are entirely eclipsed by the utter harmony of their fundamental business philosophies.

Father Joe's entrepreneurial approach to the blight of homelessness has become a model for such programs nationwide. Hardly a month passes at Father Joe's Villages without a visit from a fact-finding civic delegation hoping to replicate Father Joe's methods and his success in their town. Surprisingly (to me anyway), Father Joe's most celebrated achievement is his program's steady production of skilled line cooks, many of whom work in San Diego's finest restaurants. They are trained by former navy chefs in this port city, which takes care of the culinary end of things, but it's the program's achievements in personal redemption that are the most striking recommendation for Father Joe's approach.

Imagine going from life on the street in San Diego — where time is irrelevant, hygiene is an afterthought, and food is whatever you can beg or forage — to holding a job cooking in a four-star kitchen. Think of the complete life renovation that requires and the faith in human potential it demands. Father Joe doesn't just help his residents find jobs; he helps them reimagine their lives. An identical belief in the capacity of people to learn and to achieve informed everything Paul Jacobs told me about who Qualcomm hires and why.

"The message of our company," Jacobs professed, "is that our employees' creativity can change the world. We want people who are passionate and persistent. It's never about what they've done but how smart, flexible and creative they are. You'll find a lot of people at Qualcomm who've spent their whole careers here, and we're proud of that." If you take flexibility and teachability as synonyms, and I do, Father Joe Carroll and Paul Jacobs are speaking the same language from nearly opposite ends of the entrepreneurial spectrum. Achievement, they both insist, hinges on a willingness to learn, an appetite to improve. I call that curiosity.

While I found general agreement as to the fundamental value of intellectual hunger in business success, there was less of a consensus about how curiosity is best satisfied, and information best collected. The differences were frequently generational and, to an extent, technological.

Mike Ilitch, the founder and CEO of Little Caesars Pizza and the owner of both the Detroit Tigers and the Red Wings, had dreams of being a major league baseball player. He made it as far as minor league shortstop in the Tigers organization until a knee injury ended his career, but he put his travels with the team to good use by noting the availability (or lack thereof) of pizza in the towns he passed through in the Midwest and mid-South. Mike was a bit of a pizza fiend. He sold pies out of a Detroit nightclub in the off season and dreamed of opening his own pizzeria once he'd scraped together the seed money. In order to do that, Mike took a job offered by a buddy.

"I had a friend in sales," he recalled. "He was in the awning business, and he gave me a job getting leads for his salesmen. I went around ringing doorbells, and it was educational. I got a chance to get into people's homes and assess their values. I started getting a feel for people. When I was playing baseball, I'd sit in small towns and people watch, wonder what people did. This job let me into their lives a little. In about two years, I'd saved the $10,000 I needed to open a pizza store."

Mike performed a little domestic research as well. The father of seven children of his own, he was well aware of the considerable expense of keeping a family fed, and it was that personal experience of struggling with a household budget that helped refine his philosophy for Little Caesars. "I knew I had to make a good pizza, but I also had to give customers a good deal," he told me. "I wanted to help the household, so I was always giving stuff away. I used to give away fishing poles, ashtrays, hosiery. Ridiculous stuff, but I had a sincere feeling for the customers. I wanted to help them, and it came back to help me. We gave away all sorts of toys and trinkets, and we got a lot of business by making children happy in the arms of their mothers."

But generating sales leads with door-to-door visits is so uncommon today as to seem fanciful. It raises the question of how today's young businessperson can best gain exposure to the widest possible range of people and ideas. Those parents and mentors who want their children and charges to experience the world the way they did often have to insist upon it in strict terms. Ray Thurston, the founder of SonicAir — a highly efficient rapid delivery service purchased by UPS in 1995 — wanted his sons to know the same sort of immediate experience of life that he'd found so valuable in his youth while he worked as a messenger and delivery boy for his father. "I think my father having me work at such a young age," Ray confided, "both gave me the value of a dollar and let me see what other people's lives were like. I have two sons — 14 and 16 — and they have to start working at 15, and work all summer."

The sons, naturally enough, chafe at the imposition. "My kids complain," Ray explained, "because none of their friends work." Complaints aside, however, Ray's "program" has already produced results. "Last summer, my older boy worked with seven Hispanics on a garden crew," Ray said. "He told me he learned that the plight of a lot of people is never going to change for the rest of their lives, and he said the stories those guys told him about coming across the border and how they live here would stay with him forever."

George Argyros, one-time owner of the Seattle Mariners and America's former ambassador to Spain, had much the same experience as Ray Thurston's son but for an entirely different reason. When he was a boy, his folks were strapped for cash. "I was probably lucky my family didn't have any money because it forced me to have ambition and to work. Along the way, I met people I admired, and I kind of built a composite of who I'd like to be like, who I'd like to pattern myself after. That proved much more important to me than my academic education."

Of course, once you're embarked on a career, the trick lies in accumulating information and experience *in situ* and doing it as efficiently as possible. To that end, technology is a virtue but not an unmitigated one. It's commonplace today for twenty-somethings in business to employ their cell phones like us oldsters used to use IBM mainframes. The world is quite literally at their fingertips. They can text. They can use Twitter. They can browse the internet. They can even occasionally indulge in actual phone calls. The technology is all very liberating in its way but a little alienating as well.

Some of the friction new technology produces is generational. Many of us who didn't grow up with text

48

messaging, for instance, have cultivated a distinct preference for actual conversations. Howard Schultz falls into that category. "My kids, both in college, came home on spring break," he told me. "They came to dinner, and they put their phones on the table — laid them down like they were guns — and then they started texting. I said, 'That's it. No texting.' You would have thought I'd told them to kill somebody." It's little wonder, given the tender median age of Starbucks' workforce, that Howard Schultz has spent real time and energy figuring out how best to teach and communicate with the texting generation. "The way these kids get information — the need for instant gratification — it's very different from the way I grew up," he admitted.

Two weeks or so prior to our conversation in Howard Schultz's Seattle office, Starbucks had closed all of its American stores for an intensive employee training session. Schultz had decided that the quality of the service and the coffee had, generally speaking, fallen away from the company's impeccable standards. "I'm fond of saying if Starbucks were a twenty-chapter book, we're still only in chapter four or five," Schultz said. So the company, in his view, was experiencing a form of growing pains. "I thought the beverage quality had become mediocre at best," he confessed. "I just came in one day and said, 'We're going to close all of our stores. How long do we need to do it?' There was no research on the training session. It wasn't a financial matter. We needed to turn inward and go back to the basics, the passion we have for coffee. Of course, it was a very expensive thing to do."

Deciding to shut the doors on nearly 8,000 locations and lose three hours of business nationwide was, curiously enough, the easy part. How to conduct the training, how to convey the information, that was the challenge. Schultz had enough experience with his own children to know that they received and processed information in short bursts and weren't given to reading documents of any length. So he couldn't simply have instructions and policies drawn up and distributed to his employees, who were much more likely to be of his children's generation than his own. Schultz opted instead for a thirty-minute instructional video in which he made several cameo appearances to drive home significant points along the way.

The object was to tailor the session to the core habits of the workforce, but sometimes the adjustment is called for in the opposite direction. Robert Day, the founder and CEO of The Trust Company of the West, which manages $160 billion in assets, approaches new technology a little differently from Howard Schultz. He finds it a bit distracting, so much so that cell phones, Blackberries and the like are strictly prohibited from all meetings at The Trust Company of the West. For his part, Robert Day rarely uses a computer and is effectively inaccessible by email.

"The most important thing in life," Day insisted, "is how you deal with people. We talk about IQ," he added, "but we interview for EQ — emotional intelligence." It's Day's view that information technology, while helpful and expedient, can often get between people and serve as more of a barrier to useful interaction than a benefit. For his part, Robert Day gets his information the old fashioned way. He reads four newspapers a day. In case you're curious (I was), they are *The Financial Times, The Wall Street Journal, The New York Times,* and *The L.A. Times.*

"If you know what you're looking for," Day said, "finding information is easy. But I rarely know I'm looking for a nugget until I find it."

This sort of general hunger for information is, fundamentally, what shapes experience and drives success. Everything you've decided you don't need to know is, potentially, a missed opportunity. Dean Rasmussen, recently retired from his family's industrial construction business, passed along a scrap of wisdom he picked up from one of his mechanics. "I can," the fellow assured him, "learn something from even the dumbest son-of-a-bitch." The chances are pretty good that you can, too.

The more curious you are, the more engaged you are in what you're doing and how you're doing it — from fledgling employee to manager to entrepreneur — the further you're likely to go. Pat Fuscoe, the founder and namesake of Southern California's Fuscoe Engineering, confessed to an abiding natural curiosity about people, which has a direct bearing on how he conducts his business. "Curiosity is the lip of the funnel for me," he explained. "Once people detect my interest in them, it opens doors. A gift, a favor, a piece of information might follow. The circle starts flowing, and it goes on and on. There's a whole industry devoted to trinkets that businesses order by the thousands to give away to their customers. That might create some good will, but it's much more powerful when somebody takes a moment to get to know you."

The ultimate effect of a fully implemented sense of curiosity is heightened awareness — of facts, of circumstances, of colleagues, of competitors, of your own strengths and weaknesses. Of course, an appetite to know and a willingness to learn can't guarantee success, but what Father

Joe Carroll calls "teachability" is crucial even in failure. Peter Ueberroth — the former Commissioner of Major League Baseball, lead organizer of the Los Angeles Olympics, and *Time Magazine's* Man of the Year in 1984 — made a rather startling admission during the course of our conversation. "I've failed more than anybody I know," he said, but he quickly added, "It's all educational. When you start out doing things the right way, you think they're always going to stay right, but sometimes you fall into the pool. Just get out and dry off and learn from it."

George Fisher aired a similar sentiment. "One of the concerns I have about most young people is that they're not well prepared for the downturns, when they fail or their businesses fail or economic cycles hit," he told me. "Life is nonlinear. If you play the game long enough, you're going to have downturns. There's something called regression to the mean, which I believe in. Just make sure your mean is better than the next guy's."

A fundamental refrain running through the interviews I conducted was this: *smarten up.* Former Senator Bill Bradley — one-time small forward for the New York Knicks — has long credited both his success on the basketball court and in public life with a finely tuned "sense of where you are." In speaking with Wing Lam about the origins of Wahoo Fish Taco, he supplied a business example of the sort of awareness Bradley was referencing. "I remember asking myself," he pondered, "what's the one skill I have that nobody I know has? I knew a lot of guys who had the lineage, born to the right gene pool. That wasn't me. I had the same grades, but they had intangibles. I knew I had to find my intangible. I was in lily-white Newport Beach, and I was the only Asian kid in my high school. So I settled on the fact I was unique, and because my parents were in the restaurant business, I could cook. Me and my two brothers, we could cook. That's what we had."

Knowing where you are and who you are and what you have will likely call for a little digging on your part. The consensus opinion? Grab your shovel. Let hunger be the lip of the funnel for you as well. Always, *always*, be curious.

Lesson Two:

Always Be Persistent

"The hardest thing in business," Mike Ilitch told me, "is getting started." At the time, we were sitting in the tenth-floor conference room of the Little Caesars world headquarters in Detroit. The window over Ilitch's shoulder offered a panoramic view of Comerica Park where his Tigers play. A scant half mile away, on the north bank of the Detroit River, stood Joe Louis Arena, which Ilitch's Red Wings call home. Much of the construction and renovation in the area — conspicuous on my ride in from the airport — was either the result of Mike Ilitch's civic inspiration or his material investment. In his eighty-third year, Mike continues to have a profound effect on the city he loves and has long called home.

The present, however, seemed of little interest to him as we talked. Little Caesars was enjoying yet another record year, and the company's new veterans program, which discounts franchising fees for honorably discharged veterans and eliminates them entirely for their service-disabled brethren, was proving a considerable source of pride for the Little Caesars family of employees and cause for well-deserved public praise. Ilitch's Red Wings had advanced deep into the playoffs and were, in fact, two weeks away from taking the Stanley Cup. His Tigers were only a season removed from having won the World Series in a sweep of the St. Louis Cardinals. All things considered, the present was pretty good, but Mike preferred to focus on the past.

Generally speaking, it may be human nature to view our past personal difficulties and thorny passages through the gauzy lens of nostalgia, but the business men and women I spoke with were far more inclined to honest, clinical assessments of where they'd come from and the troubles they'd known. Accordingly, Mike Ilitch's memories of his stint collecting leads for awning salesmen and off seasons spent hustling pizzas out of the kitchen of a Detroit night club seemed far more vivid and instructive to him than the triumphs he'd enjoyed more recently. Those he'd dismiss with a wave of his hand, but the doggedness, the sense of mission and drive that had gotten him to that conference room high above resurgent Detroit, that's what mattered. That's what stayed.

After purchasing 4,000 acres of pristine land just east of Danville, CA back in 1972, Ken Behring felt as if every environmentalist, politician and government land use official was against his dream of building the high-end Blackhawk development. His vision of a turnkey neighborhood with two groomed golf courses had so much opposition that local media called it the Blackhawk Wars.

"We had all kinds of people trying to shut us down and suing us to delay building," he reflected. In a strategy to win against local opposition, Ken gifted 2,800 acres to enlarge Mount Diablo State Park and agreed to cut the development in half, down to 2,500 homes. "Five years after buying the land, my dream finally began to take shape," he commented. "That's a long time to stick with a project before the first foundation is even poured, but dreams sometimes take time, and in the end it was a huge success."

One conspicuously common feature of the stories I heard in this past year, a thread running through every interview I conducted, was this: persistence is crucial. Lasting success hinges upon it. The relentless pursuit of a dream is so obvious in some careers that it tends to go unremarked upon — Howard Schultz and his espresso bars, John Ondrasik and his hit songs, Mike Ilitch and his pizzerias, Ken Behring and his super-scale housing developments. Each qualifies as a long shot that persistence (and no little talent) brought home. But even those people I spoke to who had a leg up from the beginning needed drive and steel to reach the heights they were aiming for.

Take Robert Day, for example. His grandfather, William M. Keck, founded the Superior Oil Company in 1921. Initially a drilling contracting firm, Superior Oil would expand into exploration and partner in the construction of the first offshore drilling platform in the Gulf of Mexico in 1938. Superior Oil was acquired by the Mobil Corporation in 1984 for nearly $6 billion. The philanthropic institution established by William Keck from his Superior Oil profits remains in family control. The Keck Foundation is now a one billion dollar enterprise that supports science, engineering, and medical research throughout Southern California. The foundation not only supplies grants but funds the occasional special project like the Keck Observatory on Mauna Kea in Hawaii and the Keck School of Medicine at the University of Southern California. Robert Day currently serves as chairman and president of the Keck Foundation.

Consequently, the chances are pretty good that Robert Day would have made his mortgage whether he succeeded as an investment banker or not. While the claims of basic survival are frequently factors in success, they certainly don't have to be. The hunger to compete and win is just as powerful unmoored from practical necessity. The notion of success in business as triumph, as winning the game, was a potent recurrent theme in the conversations I had. Business isn't just business. It's personal, too.

I was struck in my conversation with Peter Ueberroth by the emotional force and vividness of his memories of rejection as a young businessman. "I came out of college at a time when I must have had 40 interviews with 40 different companies," Ueberroth recalled, "and I never got a job. I've always thought of going back one day and trying to buy those 40 companies. One of them in particular, a fiberboard company up near Tahoe." Here Peter paused and shook his head. "I really wanted that job."

He was still irritated, his enormous successes not-withstanding. Here was the man who'd organized the Los Angeles Olympics, the former commissioner of Major League Baseball, current owner (in partnership with Clint Eastwood!) of Pebble Beach, and he was still visibly irked over the failure of a Lake Tahoe fiberboard company to hire him fresh out of college. That's not sour grapes. That's persistence. That's the unebbing competitive drive on display. And that *you're making-a-mistake-if-you-don't-hire-me* attitude isn't merely what entrepreneurs and CEOs embody and exhibit routinely; it's also what they look for in their colleagues and employees.

"Attitude," George Argyros asserted, "is everything in business." I heard variations on that sentiment from virtually everyone I spoke to, including George Gorton, who is not, strictly speaking, a businessman. He's a political consultant whose career spans from the Nixon administration (he was Jeb Magruder's Watergate fall guy) through the election of Arnold Schwarzenegger. You'll find a half dozen pages devoted to George in Woodward and Bernstein's *All The President's Men*. His work hasn't been entirely domestic, and when I asked him to name the best candidate he's ever consulted for, I was surprised by the answer. "Boris Yeltsin," he said. "He was drunk and corrupt, but he wasn't evil like his opponent."

In a sense, Gorton's job is persuasion, which is hardly as concrete as, say, Howard Schultz's job of roasting and selling coffee to the world. "My mother once asked me what I did for a living," George Gorton recalled. "I said, 'I don't know. I'm in politics.'" But even if Gorton's success depends more on votes than profits, his general working philosophy and his attitude toward colleagues mirrors what I heard from people in far less exotic lines of work.

"Loyalty was very big with me when I started out," George told me. "Now it has been replaced by what's right and what's wrong. I didn't have anything to do with the Watergate break in, but if they'd said, 'Let's go bug Democratic headquarters tonight,' I'd have asked, 'What time?'" Today, as a seasoned consultant who's seen both the good and bad of politics and campaigns, Gorton approaches his job and his colleagues a bit differently.

"I took it on the chin," George mused, speaking of his Watergate days, "and now I have a sense that one has to be one's own compass. We're not cogs in a wheel but independent actors." When asked who he hires these days to work with him and why, George told me, "I look for highly motivated people. The job of the campaign is to do anything that needs to get done and do it now. The people who win are the ones who do more of the impossible than the other guys. That's how campaigns work."

George's remarks were still fresh in my mind when I interviewed Howard Schultz, who said something strikingly similar while speaking of his early years at Starbucks. "I don't think people generally realize how difficult it is to build a business," Schultz told me. "When we were losing money as a startup company, that's when we were at our best. We just willed our success. *We made the impossible possible.* We proved everyone wrong. We couldn't raise capital. Our stores were opening, and nobody cared. We had moments of great doubt but moments of great joy as well."

Of course, the ability to make the impossible possible is a byproduct of attitude, and attitude — as George Argyros has already assured us — is everything in business. So the ideal colleague, the perfect hire, is highly motivated and comes outfitted with an unerring moral and ethical compass. That is something slightly different from raw persistence. It's not enough in business just to bring energy and focus to the job you've been charged to perform. To echo George Fisher, formerly of Kodak and Motorola, good business is all about doing the right thing the right way. Paul Jacobs at Qualcomm has already told us he pays more attention to the "passion and persistence" of his employees than to their resumes, so the question becomes how to bring context to your work, how to steer by a reliable moral compass.

The key, according to Pat Fuscoe of Fuscoe Engineering, is to live your persistence. "Persistence," he stated, "is a form of consistency." Pat's advice is simple, even blunt: don't be mercenary. "Find something you're emotionally aligned with," he further explained. "Do what you do because you believe in it. That'll lead to a more productive business." As a practical matter, we can't always be doing something we love. Sometimes a job is just a job, a placeholder, and we're obliged to sell widgets. In those circumstances, it pays to remember Wing Lam's commitment to be the best dishwasher, the best busboy, the best delivery guy — to improve every job he took rather than simply perform it. In that case, Wing brought the context since the work couldn't supply it.

Pat Fuscoe's point about persistence and drive being a form of personal consistency is well taken. In the proper circumstances, with the right opportunities, what we're after fundamentally is alignment. Are we pursuing the goals we think valuable and worthwhile or are we working at cross purposes to our philosophies and our beliefs?

Scott Olivett of Oakley had quite a lot to say on this topic. "Organizations need a consistency of values," he told me. "Everybody has to be in agreement on what's important. This isn't necessarily about right and wrong. With values, there aren't always right answers. The mix varies from place to place. But organizations have to have consistency."

With a career history that ranges, most recently, from The Gap to Nike and now to Oakley, Scott has played key roles in the success of some of the best organized and best aligned organizations around. "A company is a system," he said. "It's the culmination of culture, people, infrastructure, product. You've got to understand each of those individually and all of them collectively. You need to understand strengths and weaknesses, and where you're misaligned. It's all about where you are and what you need. So I use my own framework. You need vision, strategy, a set of operating targets; you need structure, you need people, you need the culture — and you need a set of values you live by."

Of course, Scott approaches the topic from the perspective of the executive suite, but Scott's philosophy on alignment and consistency in business can be readily applied throughout the strata of any company. "At Oakley," he told me, "I tried to determine where we misaligned. I talked to employees — in the office and out of it — to try to see where we were. What were the company's historic strengths and where had we fallen behind a little bit. I also identified the things that were completely broken."

What Scott described is, effectively, curiosity married to persistence. Informed improvements are what matter in business, both top-down and bottom-up. "One of the fundamental problems of business," Scott said, "is that people now want more out of their work environment than they're getting. You see less turnover in those companies that create a good working environment and are doing something their people believe in." And turnover, according to Ray Thurston, whose SonicAir thrived on efficiency and who now consults on the topic, "is the single most important factor we measure. Anything over the 2% mark indicates a problem. Either a company isn't hiring right, or it isn't treating its people right."

Ray went on to single out Starbucks as the sort of company that treats its people right. "Starbucks depends on a small working unit, like a tribe, and the members are judged on what they do. They're self managed." Of course, this sort of independence occasionally results in mismanagement and in mistakes, but the prevailing opinion among the people I spoke to — prevailing virtually to the point of unanimity — is that it's better to get a working education from a mistake than to go through a career committed to not making waves, and doing only what is safe and predictable.

General Peter Pace was reminded of an anecdote he'd heard on the topic. "I remember hearing the story, I think from an IBM executive," the General said, "about one of his subordinates who'd made a ten million dollar mistake. His colleagues wanted the subordinate fired, but the executive asked, 'Why would I fire a guy I've just paid $10 million to educate?'"

Andrew Cherng of Panda Express offered amplification on the topic. "A mistake is something you don't do well but continue to do in the same way," he told me. "If you learn from a mistake, how bad can it be? We all make mistakes in the people we select, the decisions that we make. They're unavoidable." Andrew went on to tell me that his business was "to educate people, to build an environment where people can learn to see the possibilities of life. That's why Panda is here. Otherwise we'd have one restaurant, and I'd still be running the front desk. Okay, maybe two." Then he thought for a moment and added, "It would be a shame if I didn't know the difference between what's important and what's not important."

Miscalculations and mistakes are just part of business. They're a natural byproduct of drive and persistence. Successful entrepreneurs, managers, and employees acknowledge their mistakes and mine them for instruction. That's the only way to avoid repeating them.

Alan Schwartz, the former President of the United States Tennis Association who now builds and operates indoor tennis facilities and sports clubs, waved his hand dismissively when speaking of missteps he's made. "We all make mistakes," Alan allowed. "I've had bad clubs. I've made plenty of mistakes. I move on. Sometimes there are bigger things in life than squeezing the last dollar out of a business." He then went on to ask the crucial question. "As an entrepreneur, you're a beach ball in the ocean," Alan questioned. "Do you keep popping up when the surf washes over you?"

It helps, occasionally, if persistence, if driving forward, is your only option. When I started Life Fitness, I borrowed money from my family and friends. It totaled $450,000, and that was in 1979! I had convinced myself the world needed a $3,000 computerized exercise bike. Even if I was wrong, I had no choice but to figure out how to make it work. The persistence was all but built into the financing. I had no choice but to find a route to success.

Persistence with a purpose is the only sort of drive that matters. Blind doggedness might lead anywhere, but only informed tenacity can lead to consistency. And consistency in business, what Scott Olivett might call philosophical alignment, can be a powerful force.

Pat Fuscoe told me an illuminating story along those lines. Pat's engineering firm operates primarily in California, but Pat's environmental philosophy and his brand of personal and corporate consistency recently landed him a contract he hadn't pursued and had no reason to expect.

"If you say you care about the environment, but you're not involved, that's a problem," Pat explained. "I was environmentally inclined, and that's how I stumbled onto Miocean," he said, explaining his work cleaning up California's beaches. "Once in a blue moon, Fuscoe Engineering works outside of California. The guys who run the Montage resort — the Athens group — they like to do eco-adaptive projects. They're very luxurious. Martin Hoffman, who works for Montage, found out about this organization, Miocean, that was cleaning up California's beaches. He's a surfer. He loves the ocean, and he was looking for an organization that did good work in a low key way, and he found it in Miocean. Martin sent an email, and we invited him to our annual fundraiser. I didn't ask him for anything at all."

And that statement is key — "I didn't ask him for anything at all." The common thinking is that you're always talking when you're selling, but from my experience and from the conversations I've had, I can assure you that *listening* can be a form of selling as well, and often the more potent and effective form. We all get talked at routinely. How often are we listened to?

A couple of years passed, and then Pat gets a phone call from Montage's Martin Hoffman. "He called me up to tell about a resort they wanted to build in Costa Rica," Pat said, "and Martin asked me if my company would be interested in developing it. This was a top tier assignment, and none of it would have happened without Miocean. Martin wouldn't have noticed us. He would have probably networked around in the business community, sought proposals from big engineering firms and picked one. There's virtually no chance I would have gone after this job. There would be no pitch in the world I could have come up with that would have caused him to go with us."

In this case, Pat's alignment, his philosophy in practice, closed the deal. "By way of Miocean," Pat beamed, "Martin found out about my business accidentally and anecdotally. Not only did he select us for the job, but he made a sole-sourced decision. There was no competition, no interviews, no nothing. He went to his partners and said, 'This is the company I want to use.' That just doesn't happen."

Better still, Martin Hoffman and Montage Resorts' faith in Fuscoe Engineering has functioned for Pat as a challenge and a source of inspiration. "I'm going to do the best job possible," he assured me. "I'd never let them down. I just won't. Now that's reciprocity."

Fundamentally, Pat's experience illustrates attitude in action. In life, as well as business, it's critical that we know what we believe and why, and that we find some way to express it. It always pays to be armed with the knowledge of what we will do and what we won't do, which may require some thinking about issues we've yet to confront, situations we've so far avoided, temptations that may lie ahead. We have to decide who we are in this world and sustain uneroded confidence in that decision.

In my conversation with San Diego homeless advocate Father Joe Carroll, we spent a great deal of time talking about attitude and self-confidence as key components in human dignity. Father Joe meets people at their lowest ebb. They've lost everything, up to and including the roof over their heads. Their leading deficiency, however, isn't material. According to Father Joe, it's spiritual. "Our people need confidence," he told me. "If we're going to move them up, we want to move them up once and for all, so we start everybody out in what we call Challenge to Change, a program we run everyone through — over the objections of the government, I might add."

Challenge to Change is a thirty-day motivational program. "We try to convince our clients that they messed up their own lives," Father Joe said. "Nobody else did. The whole idea is to motivate people to change their lives and not come back. Most of our people suffer from a lack of confidence, so we have a graduation ceremony after a week. Then after two weeks. We have to get our people confident."

Only then can the clients qualify for Father Joe's comprehensive program to put them back on their feet for good.

"Our approach to homelessness used to be that they'd come in at six at night and leave at six in the morning. Our people walked the street all day. When I came here," Father Joe remembered, "I asked, 'Why don't we take them in during the day?' Of course, it took more money, but now we have an elementary school, a high school, everything on site. One stop shopping. Why shouldn't a homeless facility function that way?"

In San Diego, Father Joe's facility is commonly known as The Villages, but Father Joe has another name he prefers. "I call it the University of the Human Spirit," he said. "We run our program like a college. We give you a catalog on the services we provide, and you get points for using them. Five points if you get a pap smear. Three points if you get your teeth checked. Six points if you go to English as a second language class. It's like a typical college."

Father Joe then told me something I'd heard before in an entirely different context. "What I brought to this industry," he said, "is the concept that if you have thousands of dollars invested in someone and they fail, you still have thousands of dollars invested in them. Make it work." General Peter Pace's story of an IBM employee's ten million dollar mistake only differs in degree. The key is to guard against further failure. Find the lessons in disappointment and bad fortune. Make it work.

Of course, Father Joe is dealing with people who have failed catastrophically through bad choices, bad habits, or bad luck. His role is to build confidence (and competence) an inch at a time. In business, reversals are rarely so stark and primal, so it's more a matter of sustaining confidence and distilling the lessons in miscalculations. On this front, I had two intriguing conversations with two very different sorts of business people. One was Glen Tullman, entrepreneur and CEO of Allscripts. The other was John Ondrasik, singer/songwriter and creative force behind the band, Five For Fighting.

Glen Tullman is an accomplished amateur magician, and in 1995, at the height of the theme restaurant craze, Glen came up with an idea he called Latenite Magic. His restaurant would be a marriage of dining and legerdemain, and Glen decided to pursue as his partner the world-famous illusionist David Copperfield. Copperfield performs about five hundred shows a year all over the planet, so his audience is massive and far-flung. Consequently, once Glen had courted the magician and won him to the idea of Latenite Magic, interest in the project spiked with both the dining public and potential investors.

The Indiana insurance giant Conseco tipped in a $20 million investment, and The Walt Disney Company offered prime real estate in Orlando for the second Latenite Magic restaurant. The first would be built in New York's Times Square at the corner of Broadway and 49th Street. Plans called for a grand, 30,000-square-foot facility equipped with millions of dollars worth of specially engineered equipment that would allow for spectacular Copperfield-designed illusions to be viewed in the round. The restaurant was eighty-five percent complete, at a cost of nearly $34 million, when irreconcilable friction among the principals and a general dip in enthusiasm for theme restaurants (not to mention a host of liens and lawsuits) led to the abandonment of the project. By August of 1999, Latenite had defaulted on its Times Square rent, and the restaurant was effectively dead.

The entire forlorn misadventure was spelled out in forensic detail in a prominent article in the pages of *The New York Times*. This wasn't merely a lost investment for Glen. He'd come up with the idea originally and had pursued David Copperfield to secure his participation. The illusionist's reputation had, in turn, attracted more investors, some more problematic than others. There'd been promise of great success with restaurants not just in New York and Orlando but also Tokyo, Sydney, and London. Then the whole thing had gone kaput. The failure for Glen was both personal and professional. Worse still, it was public.

When our conversation turned to Latenite Magic, I half expected Glen to groan. Instead, he just smiled and shook his head. While I'm sure the passage of time has taken some of the edge off the disappointment, Glen's perspective on the unraveling struck me as healthy and analytical.

"Don't invest in a venture," Glen advised. "Invest in the right people." Without going into unsavory detail, Glen assured me that a few of the investors (Copperfield excepted) had behaved in ways Glen had found unconstructive, disappointing, and more than a little self-serving.

"I learned that you have to start with people," he said. "Stay away from bad people, no matter what it costs you." It was an expensive lesson, to be sure, but a lesson nonetheless, and Glen has embraced it and moved on. He never tried to tell me that Latenite Magic was a "good experiment," but he made clear that the venture was valuable to him in ways he hadn't anticipated. It was certainly an expensive education, but still an education. Glen gave every indication that, thanks to his Latenite Magic experience, he has come around to the view that good business has to be as much about people as profits.

In the sense that the failure of Latenite Magic was a personal rejection, Glen Tullman got a taste of something John Ondrasik knows a fair bit about himself. Ondrasik is a singer/songwriter and the creative force behind the band Five For Fighting. He has a couple of hit songs to his credit — *Superman* and *100 Years* — and he enjoys a productive and profitable career both as a recording artist and a performer. But his achievements haven't come easily, and perseverance has been the byword of John's career.

"I didn't have commercial success until relatively late," John told me. "I was 30 before I made any money." John was fortunate in that he had a reliable fall-back job at hand. "When my grandfather died in his mid sixties, my father took over his wire business — a welding shop in Watts called Precision Wire Products. They made oven racks and wire baskets. They had forty employees," John said. "My father brought his mechanical engineering and work ethic to the business, and now there are 300 employees. Shopping carts is their main thing. I worked there bending wire with a machine."

The word songwriters (and artists generally) hear most frequently is "no." Rejection in John Ondrasik's world is far more common than success, and fighting through the disappointment of rejection that is, by definition, personal calls for perseverance bordering on a sense of mission and unwavering self-confidence. Given the long odds of success, John calibrated his ambitions to suit the circumstances. "Early on," he confessed, "I just wanted somebody to hear a song of mine on the radio. I wanted to get paid to play somewhere. That would have been success for me."

John worked tirelessly to put himself in a position to know that success. He made his monthly nut at his father's shop. "My dad got someone with skill cheap," John observed, "and I got to go audition or go to a writing session whenever I needed to. I couldn't have done any of this without him."

As John practiced his musicianship and wrote his songs, he also attended college. "I studied math at UCLA," he said. "I thought I could get through the courses with the least possible effort and get a job when my music career imploded." At the time he had little in the way of a career to implode. "I once calculated that I worked 45,000 hours before I made a penny," John recalled. "My first royalty check was for $7. At the end of the day, it was as much about ego as making music. It was about winning. That's why I never quit."

Winning again. We can't get away from it. "I worked so hard it almost wasn't healthy, but I was obsessed with winning," John told me. He defined winning differently at various points in his career, as circumstances suited. At first he just wanted to be taken seriously as a songwriter. "I took valid criticism to heart, and it made me better," John allowed. "I've become acquainted through the years with some of the people who rejected me early on, and now I know better than to respect their judgment too much."

After he'd signed his first record deal, John's primary goal was to land another one. "When I first heard one of my songs on the radio, it was a big moment," John recalled. "Then I wanted to go onto the next moment, and the next. I never achieved the level of success I always wanted, but today I don't covet it as much as I used to."

And a substantial part of the success John has enjoyed strikes him today as almost accidental. "When I wrote *Superman*," John told me, "I thought it was a good song, but I never thought, 'This is the one!' It was just another of the thousand songs I've written." John described composing *Superman* in about forty-five minutes. "My producer stayed on me to cut it," he added. "If I hadn't, I wouldn't have this career, this life. Somehow, *Superman* got on the radio — it was too slow for the times. It shouldn't have happened, but it did. It was like drawing an inside straight." John's album *America Town,* which included *Superman,* went platinum soon after its 2000 release, selling over one million copies. For his trouble, John received a royalty check slightly in excess of $7.

John is refreshingly philosophical about his experience in the music business. "Goalposts always move," he reflected. "There's commercial success. There's artistic success — usually the opposite of commercial success. My best line will never be as good as Leonard Cohen's worst line, but he'll never be on the radio. There's something wrong with that, but that's the world we live in."

On a superficial level, John Ondrasik's profitable career as a singer/songwriter and performer can be traced to a song he tossed off in three quarters of an hour and was reluctant to record. But more fundamentally, what John has done throughout his career is put himself in a position to be successful — by working to hone his songwriting and performing skills, and by sustaining his self-confidence sufficiently to persevere through rejection. The success of *Superman* surely qualifies as the residue of design. It was anything but dumb luck.

John Ondrasik and Glen Tullman are Alan Schwartz's beach ball metaphor brought to life. When the waves wash over them, they just keep bouncing back up. It's in their natures to persevere, and when that sort of drive is married to curiosity — when the thrust is informed and savvy rather than merely antic — then the chances of success and accomplishment are exponentially improved.

Alan Schwartz told me a story about his initial attempt to build an indoor tennis facility that touched precisely upon the value of persistence in business. "I was in the industrial real estate business," Alan explained. "My dad got very ill in 1968. His doctors told him he only had a few more years to live, and we decided, as a joint effort, to build the world's largest indoor tennis club. He found a location in the city of Chicago. At that time, no indoor tennis facility had been built from scratch anywhere in the U.S. A number of cities had converted buildings, but no one had actually built from the ground up.

"Seventeen Chicago banks turned us down for a loan. These were all banks that had lent me money for industrial real estate projects, but they forgot my name when I came to talk about an indoor tennis club. There wasn't even zoning for such a thing in Chicago at the time. Then I read an article in *Time Magazine* about a guy named Donald Parsons who'd been to high school and college with me. It said in the article he'd just taken over the Bank of the Commonwealth of Detroit where he was known as a maverick, and he was upsetting the bankers there.

"So I picked up the phone and called him," Alan continued. "I told him what I needed, told him about all the other banks that turned me down, and he invited me to come out to Detroit. He didn't want to see any projections, any renderings, a presentation. Nothing. He said, 'What do you need?' I said I needed a loan to start of $900,000. He said, 'You've got it.'"

Alan was flabbergasted. "I asked him why he'd do such a thing with no collateral, no nothing. He told me when I was playing varsity tennis at Yale he used to watch my matches, and he knew I'd kill myself before I'd lose. He knew I'd do the same thing before I'd go bad on his loan. I remember he said, 'It won't be long before the other bankers will want to take the business away from me.' It worked out just that way."

Today, Alan invests in startup businesses and so is in much the same position of his former classmate in Detroit. "I look for commitment in young entrepreneurs," Alan told me. "I'm making my own judgment if they'll fold up the tent when it's really dark. Sure, you look at the idea, but the person is more important than the idea."

Toward the end of our conversation, Alan was reminded of something his father had once told him. "He said I could learn from every loss. That losing doesn't make you a loser. That failing," Alan added, "doesn't make you a failure."

In the same vein, it's useful to understand that success is a process with a wealth of moving parts and some good fortune involved. Setbacks and disappointments, outright rejection — they're all part of the game. As I've grown increasingly fond of saying since my diagnosis with ALS, you can't control what happens to you, but you can control how you respond to it. The same is true in business. We've already established active curiosity as a virtue in the workplace, but the appetite to learn and to master is only effective when joined with drive and a dedicated sense of perseverance.

Dr. Jeffrey Trent, the CEO of the genomic research laboratory TGen, told me something he'd heard from a jogging buddy of his, a former congressman from Kansas. "In the Congress," Jeffrey articulated, "the answer to the question 'Do I have your support?' is usually 'I'm with you as long as I can be.' Think of the difference between people who are with you to the end," Jeffrey said, "and those who are with you as long as they can be. I want the ones with me to the end."

Don't we all. In business, as in life, curiosity matters, but perseverance pays. Stay to the end. Always be persistent.

Lesson Three:

Always Be Strategic

Of course, even the most scrupulously informed persistence won't do you much good if you don't know where you're going. Curiosity and devoted energy are of little use without an objective, without a strategy.

By the time Cookie Lee started her jewelry business in her spare bedroom, she'd held several high-powered corporate jobs, including stints with Mattel, Johnson & Johnson, and Beatrice Foods, where she served as marketing director for Orville Redenbacher popcorn. So Cookie had firsthand knowledge of the demands of the corporate treadmill when she began contemplating going out on her own. Having grown up as a latchkey kid, the daughter of two working parents, Cookie craved a different experience for her children, and for herself as a mother.

"I started the business in 1985," she told me, "hoping I'd be able to work out of the house and raise the kids." That was her strategy. That was her objective. Even today, with many thousands of consultants depending on Cookie for their livelihoods and with annual sales in excess of $100 million, Cookie has never lost sight of her initial goal. As a result, she's created a decidedly family friendly business. "We try to make sure our employees have family time," Cookie said, "and I think that's why women join our company. Our business is like a giant sorority. Our 100,000th consultant just signed up about a week ago,"

Cookie noted in the spring of 2008. "That's a lot of people, the size of a city. It's important for me to get to know them and talk to them. When you get big, that gets harder and harder to do." She went on to say, with heartfelt pride, "My very first consultant is still with me. I met her in Junior League. She and I were sitting next to each other, and we started talking."

In person, Cookie Lee is conspicuously energetic, enthusiastic, irrepressible. But she is also a highly disciplined businesswoman with a reliable sense of what's important in her company, what's important in her life, and the necessary interplay between the two. Corporate structures, no matter their scale, tend toward ossification. Too many layers. Too many managers. Too many teams and divisions. Too many meetings. Way too many meetings, all too often conducted out of habit rather than necessity.

At Cookie Lee Jewelry, the founder, lead designer, and head cheerleader is committed simultaneously to fun *and* efficiency. While she wants her staff and her consultants to take the pleasure in the business that she takes in it, she also insists they stay mindful of the fundamental objective of Cookie Lee Jewelry, which is the agreeable marriage of happy customers and efficient employees. Consequently, Cookie is frequently prompted to ask the same question at company meetings she attends: what are we trying to achieve today? "It's easy to lose sight of that," Cookie admitted. "I take big post-its and stick them to the wall during a meeting so we can keep track of what we're doing, why we're there. It's easy to forget what the objective is."

Strategy, by definition, is the thread of business. It's the plot of a successful enterprise. Good strategists practice the art of keeping the objective in sight. If you don't always know why you're doing what you're doing — as an entrepreneur, as an executive, as a manager, as an employee — you're sure to drift and likely to be aimless, unproductive, and inefficient. So the challenge lies in developing a simple, effective professional strategy that you can both abide by and thrive with. The crucial question is *how* do you want to do what you do — and implied in the *how* is the *why*. Cookie Lee, for instance, wants to keep her jewelry business fun and focused because it started as a hobby specifically intended as an antidote to the occasional drudgery and near bottomless demands of corporate life. So Cookie is keen on efficiency — less time on business, more time for family.

When my conversation with General Peter Pace turned to the topic of strategy, I was surprised by the similarity of his approach to Cookie's. General Pace's strategy has Cookie Lee's "What are we trying to do today?" feel to it. During his leadership years, Pace subjected each of his substantial orders and Pentagon directives to the same test: how will this affect Private Pace? (Private Pace is the General's grunt version of himself.)

"Private Pace reminds me and everybody around me that the decisions we make will have an impact on real people," the General told me. "PFC Pace automatically transports all of us onto the battlefield. Private Pace has always kept me focused on the responsibility I had to take care of the young guys and gals who are our PFCs and Lance Corporals. And he allowed me in a gentle but straightforward way to remind everybody else around the table here in Washington — in a nice air-conditioned room with good lighting — that our decisions would have an impact on real people."

The notion of Private Pace, as it turned out, took hold with the General's colleagues at the Pentagon. "After I used Private Pace multiple times when I was Vice Chairman," he recalled, "people started asking me, 'How's this going to affect PFC Pace?' I liked that. It meant they were thinking straight."

The General was aided by the fact that Private Pace, for him, wasn't just a convenient construct but was a real soldier, an early version of the man Peter Pace had become. As a raw lieutenant tossed into the caldron of the Tet offensive in Hue City in 1968, Peter Pace had endured the Private Pace experience up close and all too personal. He knew firsthand the challenges soldiers face in battle, and he'd been well-schooled in the value of calm consistency, both in the rear and at the front. "If you stay calm," the General told me, "no matter what's happening, the best that can happen will likely happen." General Pace is a firm believer in personal consistency as a means of reigning in a fractious world. "How you react to events impacts the event itself and everyone around you," he insisted. "My guys in Vietnam would say, 'We're up to our ass in alligators here, but the lieutenant is calm. He's laughing. It's going to be okay.' It was all self-discipline. I had fear, and my stomach was churning," the General confessed. "Under fire, you learn a lot about yourself. I knew I'd be scared, and I was. Every time I got shot at, I got scared. If you shoot at me today, I'll be scared today. It never goes away."

The key for General Pace lay in controlling the fear, in learning from it. He knew from experience what Private Pace would likely be up against in theater, so as he ascended through the ranks, finally reaching the pinnacle of the Chairmanship of the Joint Chiefs of Staff, General Pace never lost site of his objective, never swerved from his fundamental strategy to always perform in the best interest of PFC Pace. The layers of responsibility may have shifted with each promotion in rank and each new job, but Peter Pace's core duty to Private Pace never did.

At my urging, Peter Pace offered up a general lesson on the shape of strategy in the armed forces. "From the military standpoint," he said, "strategy is crafted both in Washington and at the regional level. Tactics are done on the battlefield. Generically, the strategy is the vector you're on — to build something, to take something down. The strategy for Iraq, for instance, is to help the Iraqi government to grow its own armed forces to take care of its own responsibilities so we can come home and leave a relatively stable country behind that can take care of itself.

"The guys on the ground are trying to figure out day to day how to control their sectors of Baghdad in a way that will either let the Iraqis have leadership or let us work side by side, so that eventually they're in the lead with us gone. The lieutenants," General Pace said, "the captains and the majors are working a block-by-block strategy, while General Petreus (supreme commander in Iraq at the time) is working the province by province strategy. The Centcom Commander is looking at Iraq and Afghanistan and the rest of his region and the Joint Chiefs are looking at the globe."

But even with global responsibility as the Chairman of the Joint Chiefs of Staff — perhaps *because* of that global responsibility — Peter Pace took it as his job to be calm and non-confrontational, to be steady and fixed on his objective of serving Private Pace. "I came to be known as Dr. Valium," he confessed, "because I always tried to be the guy who was hearing past the yelling and trying to find a solution. When folks try to push you off your spot," the General added, "mentally or physically, don't get pushed off. Allow yourself to be convinced off, but if you shouldn't move off, don't move."

One very public example of General Pace's unwillingness to be pushed off his spot came during a televised press briefing where General Pace shared the podium with his boss, Secretary of Defense Donald Rumsfeld. A reporter asked the men to speak to the responsibilities of soldiers who witness the abuse of Iraqi detainees. General Pace stated unequivocally, "It's absolutely the responsibility of every U.S. service member, if they see inhumane treatment being conducted, to intervene to stop it."

Donald Rumsfeld interjected with what he intended as a clarification. "I don't think you mean," he remarked, "they have an obligation to physically stop it. It's to report it."

Pace's response came as a surprise to the reporters in the room and to Rumsfeld as well. "No sir," he said. "If soldiers are physically present when inhumane treatment is taking place, they have an obligation to try to stop it."

As General Pace explained to me, his stark disagreement with his boss in front of a roomful of reporters and a bank of television cameras was a direct result of his core philosophy, his fundamental strategy to think first and foremost of Private Pace.

"I was asked a question at a news conference," the General told me, "on nationwide TV and transmitted into the combat zone, so I understood my words were going to be heard. I said it was the responsibility of every U.S. service member, if they saw abuse on the battlefield, to stop it if it was in their power. Secretary Rumsfeld said what he thought

I meant to say was . . . something different. I said, 'No, that's not what I meant. What I meant to say was what I did say, which is we expect American service men to stop abuse of anybody on the battlefield.'"

That was the end of the matter for public consumption, but I wondered what had transpired once the men had left the podium and the glare of the TV lights. "It was not a pleasant moment for me to publicly push back at my boss," General Pace admitted. "On the other hand, I knew exactly what I was doing, and I knew it was much more important that PFC Pace on the battlefield get the exact, correct, straight message than it was that I appear to be subordinate to the Secretary of Defense on TV."

In other words, General Pace was well aware that the consistency of his strategy, of his principles, took precedence over the discomfort of the moment. General Pace confessed that his remarks had a lingering effect on his relationship with Secretary Rumsfeld. "After that news conference, he and I were okay," Pace said, but added, "I think the more he thought about it, the less comfortable he was. My words were in exact agreement with the orders on the street, so I was satisfied I'd done the right thing even though it meant, for a little while, the comfort level between me and my boss was less than I would have liked it to be."

The warm tone and color of General Pace's remarks about Donald Rumsfeld made it unambiguous that his public disagreement with the man hadn't been in any way personal but was instead entirely strategic. General Pace had simply been keeping his objective in sight, and his objective (as always) was Private Pace. To get back to the question Cookie Lee poses in every meeting — "What are we trying to achieve today?" — the General was trying to make PFC

Pace understand his responsibilities on the battlefield — what PFC Pace should do that day and every day when it came to Iraqi detainees. That the General was wholly comfortable airing his opinion in such a public forum he credits to Donald Rumsfeld who, according to Pace, invited dissent as a means of formulating his own strategies.

"Secretary Rumsfeld was a world-class wrestler in college," General Pace recalled. "If he could pin you, he had no respect for you. He liked the mental contact. He liked the challenge. He would come into a room and say, 'Here's the problem, let's talk about it.' If you weren't talking when you were with him, you were wasting space, and you weren't invited back. The people he promoted had pushed back."

Pace, by his own admission, pushed back quite a bit. "The Secretary was always very comfortable with me because I would break his chops in public," Pace said. "My view was, if I was going to have a career-ending joke, it had better be a good one. Mr. Rumsfeld liked to have me in the room because he knew I'd say what was on my mind."

In Peter Pace's view, Donald Rumsfeld's approach to developing strategy and refining objectives had much to recommend it. "Be a strong advocate for what you believe is correct," the General clarified, "but realize there are always other factors at work. Understand that and accept it. Then you can very comfortably put things on the table and challenge ideas up until the time the decision is made. After that, go out and execute that decision, whether you agree with it or not."

Donald Rumsfeld might have had a dictatorial reputation with the press and the public, but General Pace revealed that the truth about Rumsfeld's approach to thorny strategic issues was something different than was popularly imagined.

"Once Secretary Rumsfeld had conviction about something," General Pace said, "he'd go public and say, 'This is what we're going to do.' But to get there, there was a lot of back and forth."

The back and forth, the challenges, the arguments, the asking and answering of what may seem to be simple, fundamental questions is what perfecting a strategy is all about. Without an ongoing examination of means and motives, a tireless weighing of possibilities, you can't be certain of what you haven't thought of, can't know what you don't know. In the words of General Pace's former boss, this world is rich with both known unknowns and unknown unknowns, so in business it's always better to be humble and flexible in the face of near limitless possibility.

"I've lived my life thinking outside the box," mused Ken Behring, who has created major shifts in his business ventures almost every decade since first selling his life insurance policy as a youngster to buy a bike for delivering cheese in the morning and newspapers in the afternoon. "Making money was my main goal so I remained open to the next best opportunity."

From car sales to real estate development, Ken shifted into owning a professional football team, buying the Seattle Seahawks from the Nordstrom family. "Joe Nordstrom wanted $80 million for the team but gave me a 'deal' for $79 million," Ken recounted. "I certainly hadn't intended to buy the Seahawks when I flew up to Washington, and just maybe Joe Nordstrom was even a better salesman than I was," he quipped. "But when an opportunity presents itself, your decision has to be part business and part gut instinct."

Oakley's Scott Olivet put it this way: "I always figure I'm 50% right. Better to test my theories, and I'll change my view." Of course, there are all sorts of ways to test theories, some more productive (and less painful) than others. George Fisher told me about one of his theory-testing experiences at Motorola. "We built a plant in Texas, and we thought it was our chance to do everything new and do it right," he explained. "It turned out it was too much, and the project nearly collapsed. We had new factories, new systems, new products — all at one time. Our computers were backed up with generators, and everything worked fine until the power went out one day. Somebody had forgotten to buy diesel fuel to run the generators, and we lost all of our data from that one mistake."

George Fisher was a thirty-six-year-old executive at the time, and his experience in that Texas blackout stayed with him for the rest of his career, not just at Motorola but at Kodak as well. "Did anybody buy the diesel fuel? I've asked that question many times since then," George admitted. "Just because a bunch of things are right doesn't mean a company has the organization or the bandwidth to pull them off all of at once. It's always okay to ask simple questions. There's nothing wrong with that."

Mike Gray learned a similar lesson at Sweet Life. Early in the company's existence, when the business was struggling to grow and establish itself well beyond its modest retail bakery roots, Mike was informed by his banker, "You don't have enough horsepower in your accounting department." Initially, he didn't quite know what to make of the remark. "In the beginning," Mike told me, "I only hired people I could afford, thinking I'd save money here and there. I didn't hire the best talent available, people who'd be able to operate into our growth. But as soon as I started hiring ahead of the curve, employees began coming to me with stuff I hadn't thought about."

As to the lack of horsepower in the accounting department? "Once we had enough horsepower," Mike said, "I knew what the guy meant. We went from being tactical to being strategic." Mike had finally brought on board the sort of people who knew to buy the diesel fuel.

So strategy can hinge, in some instances, on forward thinking — on hiring ahead of the curve — but personal history can also serve as a key resource in developing a viable business strategy. Sometimes it simply pays to keep your eyes open and digest what you see. Wing Lam's "did anybody buy diesel fuel?" moment came while he was still a busboy at his family's Chinese restaurant in Southern California. "My parents owned the Pine Garden on Balboa Island," Wing told me. "One of my dad's regular customers, Gloria Zigner, was a publicist, and the story everybody knows is that she threw a birthday party for John Wayne at the restaurant, and my dad sang happy birthday to him. From that point on, you couldn't get a table at the restaurant. There was a two-hour wait to get in. Everybody had their birthday parties there. They would sit at the table where John Wayne sat, and my dad would come out in his chef's hat and sing this song in Chinese, which had nothing to do with birthdays or John Wayne. It was very strange."

Only many years later did Wing discover the truth behind the legend. "Gloria Zigner recently met my brother," he said, "and she told him the real story. She was John Wayne's wife's publicist, and she was actually throwing a birthday party for her husband. She asked John Wayne's wife to stop by with *her* husband. They stopped in for a few minutes, and my dad had his picture taken with John Wayne. That's it, and it made the restaurant."

Wing distilled a valuable lesson from the whole affair. "I learned," he mused, "that people are star struck." And he learned it in the context of the restaurant business, so when Wing and his brothers opened the first Wahoo's Fish Taco, Wing knew one thing for sure: "I knew we needed our John Wayne."

Star power would be to Wahoo's in California what diesel fuel was to Motorola in Texas. It would make everything work. Celebrity presence, Wing understood, could do more than simply enhance success; it could create it. The Lam brothers, all passionate surfers, had established their cuisine and organized their restaurant around the vibe of the beach, so Wing knew instinctively that their John Wayne should be a world-class surfer.

There were a half dozen surf clothing manufacturers in the immediate area of the first Wahoo Fish Taco, and Wing set his informal John Wayne hunt in motion with the help of a rep from Billabong. "One of their guys came into our shop," Wing recalled, "maybe six weeks into our business. He noticed our employees wore just shorts and T-shirts to work, and he asked if we wanted to do a walkthrough of their warehouse. I did the walkthrough and got a pair of shorts and a T-shirt and a hat for each of our employees. They were big on day-glo colors at the time. You couldn't miss the stuff.

"It was maybe three days later when the head marketing guy from Quicksilver came in, and he said he couldn't be served by somebody wearing his competitor's clothes. So off I go to his warehouse." In addition to the clothing, Wing began to collect stickers and even the odd surfboard — all of them freely given — which he displayed on the walls of his restaurant. Wing then bought the entire back cover of *O P Pro,* a magazine devoted to the world's most prestigious surfing competition. "I went around and asked to use the logos of the surf clothing manufacturers in our neighborhood," Wing recalled. "There were six of them at the time, and they all said Wahoo could be their official restaurant."

"The next year," he added, "we ran the same ad along with a picture of the top surfer and the 'staff behind the man.' After that, every kid who surfed came into the restaurant, and the pros were there too. They were all there. So I didn't have one John Wayne. I had a John Wayne here. A John Wayne there. John Waynes all over the place.

"If you surf," Wing said, "Wahoo is your food. That was our approach." The strategy has yielded spectacular results to date. One hundred restaurants across the country, $150 million in annual sales, and a kind of sports cache — with professional athletes both as regular customers and investors — that Wing could only have dreamed of when he collected those first day-glo T-shirts. Now, skiers, skateboarders, and baseball and football players frequent and, in some instances, own pieces of Wahoo restaurants. And it all started with John Wayne's wife's publicist's husband's birthday party.

The strategy Wing and his brothers developed preceded their business, and the success of Wahoo Fish Taco has depended, in large part, on their willingness to stick to that initial strategy in its purest and most effective form. Though he was inspired by the John-Wayne-birthday phenomenon at his parents' Balboa Island restaurant, Wing Lam made one significant addition to the equation: authenticity. He wanted his John Waynes — his sportsmen and sportswomen — to be real and devoted customers of Wahoo Fish Taco for an exceedingly practical reason, a reason explained best by Scott Olivet of Oakley. "Kids today smell poseurs a mile away," he told me. "They understand how commercials work. They understand how endorsements work. You're not fooling anybody. If your market is teenagers or people who are core to sport, to technology, anything — they know authenticity when they see it."

So it matters that Wahoo's John Waynes aren't simply extreme sport superstars but are also authentic patrons of the restaurant chain and its beach-aesthetic cuisine. They use the product, actually and authentically. In that respect, Wing and his brothers updated the lucky happenstance that helped make their parents' restaurant a birthday destination. In essence, they formulated a strategy based on observation and experience and then went about pursuing it. In business, as in life, it's far more common for circumstances to dictate strategy rather than the other way around. More usually, an effective business strategy is born of tireless tinkering and hard won real world experience over time. The massive grocery chain Safeway serves as an instructive case in point.

I had the pleasure of sitting down with Safeway CEO Steve Burd for a couple of hours to find out what it's like to run a company with nearly 1,800 stores, a quarter of a million employees, and over 30 million customers a week. Burd has been in the job for a remarkable 15 years, an unusually long stint for a chief executive, and he has seen Safeway grow both in scope and mission during that time. Safeway has long been involved in charitable giving, more for humane purposes than strategic ones, but what started as a peripheral activity has become central to the company's strategy for continued business success. According to Steve Burd, Safeway has found that it can do well by doing good.

"When I joined the company," Steve told me, "Easter Seals was our major charitable cause. We'd give money and food to food banks, and we did other things on a very local basis. Given the number of customers in and out of our stores every week, we knew that failing to engage in community giving would be foolish. We always want to be part of the fabric of the communities we serve. Twelve-year-olds today might someday come to work for us, and they'll make their decisions on where to work based on what kind of company we are. So our philanthropy is an advantage, and it excites our employees." Steve Burd went on to tell me that the "difference in great morale and poor morale can be a 5% difference in sales. We want our employees to enthusiastically embrace what we do, why we do it, and who we are."

In part, then, Safeway's company-wide involvement in philanthropy was a strategic move intended to position the stores favorably in the communities they serve and help cement the loyalty and focus the enthusiasm of Safeway's employees. As the company's general habit of philanthropy evolved, the fundraising efforts became more directed and more thoughtful. "For raising money," Steve Burd commented, "nothing is more efficient than a supermarket. It just takes a couple of seconds in a check stand. We feel obligated to use our efficiency for the greater good, so we pick causes we feel we can and should focus on." Safeway's initial and scattershot practice of raising money for scout troops and volunteer firemen — for just about any cause or organization a store manager deemed worthy — yielded gradually over time to a more strategic approach to fundraising. "A check here and check there doesn't change the world, so we decided to focus, company wide, and take full advantage of our assets."

For years, Safeway had partnered with Easter Seals in a concerted annual fundraising effort, but as the grocery chain developed a more comprehensive corporate interest in philanthropy, Steve Burd and his colleagues began to cultivate a greater appetite for directing where and how the money they raised was spent. "With Easter Seals, we'd write one check, and it was over with. We were putting a lot of effort into raising the money, but it wasn't really connected to Safeway. We decided we wanted to be more involved in how the money was used."

To that end, Safeway began to identify social ills and diseases it wanted to specifically assist through its fundraising prowess. This was the exact reverse of how the company had started in philanthropy. "The scouts would come to us and ask for $100," Burd recalled, "and we'd give it to them." Once Burd began to see Safeway's philanthropic clout as a potent strategic tool — and a social responsibility the company's approach changed. Safeway began identifying significant targets for its funding, starting with cancer. "It was a conscious decision to pick cancer, the nation's number two killer," Steve told me, "because it has probably touched the lives of all of our employees and all of our customers."

Institutionally, Safeway took the view that their substantial support of leading-edge cancer research might well result in a cure for the disease, and the passion for doing good not just for the company but for humanity generally proved to be infectious. Safeway's vendors wanted to be involved as well once Safeway made it known that their intent was nothing short of eradicating cancer, with a specific emphasis on helping to develop new treatments for breast cancer and prostate cancer. "Our vendors have been anxious to help," Steve assured me. "Most of them don't have the same opportunity in their companies, so this is their chance to play. What really helps with vendor support is that everyone wants to be part of something bigger than themselves."

That certainly applies to Safeway's customers as well, particularly when they can be sure that their donations are finding the intended targets efficiently and effectively. So it was in everybody's strategic interest for Safeway to become something more than a mere fundraising goliath. In speaking of the company's philanthropic efforts, Steve Burd clarified that Safeway hadn't gone into fundraising "with the intention of getting a return on investment, but then we started to get very involved in how the money was used. We wanted to understand the research. We wanted to see the results."

As an institution, Safeway has come a long way from checks to scout troops. "We've recently bought mammography units for Alaska, Seattle, Nevada, Texas, and northern California," Steve mentioned. "These units are designed to go into neighborhoods to give mammograms. It takes 15 minutes rather than half a day. We want to know how many people use the unit and what the results are. We want to make sure they serve as many people as possible." Moreover, the emphasis on curing disease, on the health of the nation at large, has had a profound effect on Safeway's institutional understanding of the needs of its employees where healthcare is concerned.

As Steve Burd revealed to me, the evolution of his company's healthcare philosophy was spurred in significant part by sheer dollars and cents. "As a company, we've certainly gotten deeply engaged in healthcare," Steve observed, "but we sort of backed into it. We're self-insured, and our healthcare costs are around one billion dollars annually. That cost rises 10% a year." So the sheer expense of insuring its employees proved a significant incentive for Safeway's ongoing interest in eradicating disease even if the company's annual health insurance spend hadn't factored initially into the thrust and direction of Safeway's fundraising efforts. That Safeway's internal corporate interest and the general theme of its fundraising have recently dovetailed into a cohesive focus on the nation's health is largely a case of happy coincidence becoming refined corporate strategy.

The longstanding motto of the company is *Ingredients for Life*. "That's why it's so important for us to be engaged in anything that has to do with people's health and the quality of their lives," Steve added. "We think the awareness we build among the population is as important as the money we raise, and we firmly believe the connection between what we do and the communities we serve will happen over time."

For Safeway, the engagement with people's health begins with their own employees. The advancing expense of insuring the Safeway workforce has seen to that. But Safeway's longstanding interest in the health of the nation has supplied the company with an informed perspective and an expertise that has allowed Steve Burd and his colleagues the latitude to come up with something entirely new in health coverage. "We decided if we could alter our employee's behavior, they'd have better lives and we'd have lower costs," Steve explained. "We've subsidized memberships in fitness centers around the country for our employees. Smokers at our company pay a higher insurance premium. We charge people more for having, say, a 35 body mass index, but if they improve that, we'll rebate the premiums they've paid. We don't want to punish our employees," Steve insisted. "We want them to be healthier. Some people think we've invaded our employees' privacy a little, but they tolerate it because our approach is so holistic."

The fundamental object of Safeway's approach is to both encourage good health and treat illness aggressively. With far too many companies, the insurers throw up obstacles to speedy, effective treatment as a means of cost cutting. Safeway bucks that trend. Steve Burd and his healthcare brain trust have come up with a concierge service for Safeway's employees. An employee diagnosed with an illness, such as some form of cancer, is effectively taken by the hand by one of Safeway's health care concierges who educates the employee about his treatment and walks him through every stage of it. "The irony of this concierge service," Steve told me, "is when you provide the expertise and have better outcomes, everybody wins. Our employees get a longer, better quality of life and it costs less money."

That's right. It's not just more effective; it's cheaper. Furthermore, the inventive Safeway approach to healthcare has had a profound effect on the Safeway workforce. "If you really want to build loyalty," Steve said, "you help an employee with a medical problem." And Burd is certainly in a business that has seen troubled relations between management and labor in the past few years. "We've had nine labor strikes in the past fifteen years," Steve recounted, "but because of the rising cost of healthcare and our efforts to control it, we have a completely different relationship with our unions today. We have a common goal with our unions. They think we're rational people."

Steve is convinced that Safeway's approach to healthcare can be readily exported and may well be the key to solving what has become a national crisis in health coverage. "We think if you take the Safeway behavior-driven healthcare solution to heart," Burd explained, "the national healthcare bill will drop by 40%. That would free up a lot of money for research. I've already talked to fifty U.S. senators about healthcare. Safeway has become an example of what can be done, and we have to show the politicians the way."

Steve Burd's plans for Safeway-style health coverage are ambitious but seem, with each passing month, to be more attainable. "I want 30 companies in the next 12 to 18 months to sign on to what we did at Safeway," Steve said, "and we'll go to Washington and write the national policy. We have a will to win, and that's the way you have to approach everything."

The best strategies — and Safeway's strikes me as one of them — serve business and something greater simultaneously, because good strategic business thinking is both about profit and the world at large. Just like you and me, corporations are citizens, and good citizenship matters.

Ken Behring described his signature Blackhawk development as a "win" for everyone because of being a good citizen in the community where he now resides with his wife, Pat, in their 30,000-square-foot home.

Because Ken was willing to make concessions, "the environmentalists won and the county and state governments won, and the homeowners who now live in elegant homes have won." Ken Behring kept the good of Blackhawk's community neighbors in mind as he realigned his

Lesson Four:

Always Be Honorable

I recently had an impromptu lesson in old-style customer relations, the sort of experience that made me all the more appreciative of the enlightened, conscientious approach to business practices that is the focus of this book. After a dozen years with the same internet service provider — we'll call it Earthlink — I'd decided to consolidate and update my various addresses and accounts. My plan was to go with a new local company that was offering the services I needed at bargain rates. Foolishly, I thought it would be a simple matter to cancel my outdated dial-up account. I'd been a good Earthlink customer, and while I thought I might be offered a few incentives to stay on, I didn't anticipate much bother in ending our relationship.

So I went to the Earthlink website and began scouring for the proper instructions that would lead me to the form or supply me with the phone number I'd need to close out my account. After a good forty-five minutes of searching, I was no more clued in than I'd been when I started. There was plenty of information about opening accounts and upgrading them but nothing about closing one. I then turned to a Google search, where I discovered scores of fellow travelers, people determined to close their accounts for one reason or another but at an abject loss as to how that might be done. I found a few confident suggestions that all one needed to do was call this number or fax that number and development plans. He and his family have made this housing project their home, and are engaged and generous residents. Ken planted more than 400,000 trees in the original community to create a secluded and secure area. "Today these trees have matured, the golf courses have hosted national tournaments, and the waterways we created are beautiful," he added.

Mike Gray, when speaking of his experience at Sweet Life, managed to boil down the key element of sound strategy to a solitary question: "What's your sugar cookie?" Sweet Life made a lot of confections, but Mike Gray never lost sight of the fact that the sugar cookie was, far and away, the bakery's biggest seller. Safeway's sugar cookie? Their employees. The medical innovation that Safeway has helped fund, the many causes the company has supported through the years — these good works are only made possible by money raised at the check stands by Safeway's checkers. The employees are the company's prime link to the public, and their enthusiasm and commitment matter. Keeping them satisfied and loyal, ensuring their health and happiness, isn't just good karma; it's good business.

It's also good strategy. Smart. Efficient. Practical. *Profitable*. The bottom line is this: it pays to be strategic. Always be strategic.

everything would be settled in a flash. So I called and I faxed, but nothing happened. And by "nothing," I mean my ISP continued to dock me twenty dollars a month for a service I no longer wanted or used. My old dial-up account was the thing that wouldn't die.

I got distracted by business, by life, and chose for a while to believe that the wheels at Earthlink just turned very, very slowly — that my calls and my fax would take effect at length. I was convinced I'd soon check my Visa bill and there'd be no $19.95 charge for internet access I hadn't used in years. Then six months went by, and I awoke one morning sufficiently exasperated to apply myself to driving a stake through my dial-up account's relentless heart. Enough was enough. Another search. More confident misinformation. And then something new and useful from a former Earthlink customer.

At the time, I wasn't entirely convinced there could be such a thing as a *former* Earthlink customer. This gentleman — he went by Mooshu — had graced a forum to pass along the sweet, secret knowledge of how a mere mortal might divorce Earthlink. Forget calling and faxing. Earthlink, as it turned out, was much more proper and Victorian than that. The company required a registered letter to the Atlanta home office, a letter containing every scrap of pertinent information bearing upon the account along with the customer's stated request that the account be closed once and for all.

I wrote the letter. I carried it to the post office and paid to register it. I sent it. Three months later, the account was no more.

I would like to believe there is some constructive purpose for this policy, that it's intended to ward off cyber hoodlums who maliciously close dial-up accounts from their lawless strongholds on barges in the Caspian Sea. Or maybe customers had been given to such rampant accidental account closings that Earthlink had begun insisting on registered letters to protect us from ourselves. In the end, however, I decided the answer was much more straightforward and a lot less flattering to Earthlink: the company simply wanted my money more than they wanted my business. I was a monthly payment to Earthlink, and that's all that mattered. In the year it took me to close the account, I was never provided any incentive to stay on but only a tortured path to departure. Looking at it now, the process seems all but designed to create disaffected customers. That's one hell of a business model.

I was reminded of my Earthlink experience as I sat in Howard Schultz's Seattle office, where he showed me a photo of a Great Dane. The dog's name was Cooper, and the picture had come to Schultz via email from a regular Starbucks customer in Grand Rapids, Michigan. She had written that she often drives with Cooper in the back seat of her car, and when she stops at her local Starbucks drive-thru for coffee, Cooper is routinely given a small cup of whipped cream as a complimentary treat. The dog, it seems, has developed the habit of yelping with delight whenever he sees the Starbucks logo. Now that's an enthusiastic and spontaneous endorsement very unlike the shiver of contempt I feel whenever I think of Earthlink. Which response is the better business goal?

What I noticed commonly among the people I interviewed was a determination to run their businesses from a customer or a client's perspective. I recall a regular segment on Michael Moore's short-lived TV show when he would challenge CEOs of major American corporations to unpackage or assemble products their companies sold. Items encased in nearly impenetrable plastic clamshells. Objects lacquered with unnecessary and all but irremovable stickers. Disassembled furnishings shipped with such sketchy instructions that putting them together was a matter of rank guesswork. Moore's object, as always, was to demonstrate how out of touch with day-to-day reality corporate muckety-mucks can be. Almost inadvertently, however, the segment frequently begged a larger question. What is the fundamental purpose of business? Manufacturing most specifically but all commerce generally. Is the goal just to get widgets out the door? To make the sale? To close the deal? Or is there a responsibility beyond that? What, in short, does a business owe its customers and clients in return for their patronage?

My interview subjects proved to be tuned into this question, and not just as entrepreneurs and executives but as consumers, as customers, as clients. I know from my own experience that in the executive suite, you can't afford to forget what it's like on the showroom floor. Early on in the production of the Life Cycle, I met with ample opportunity to sift through customer input and empathize with disappointed health club owners who could only function successfully with the sort of stout, reliable equipment that we were laboring to provide them. Our goal was the same as theirs — an exercise bike that would hold up under hard use — and my job was to make sure our customers were still around when we could supply the rugged, perfected bike that they wanted and we wanted for them.

To that end, I insisted on an unconditional guarantee that applied to every piece of equipment we sold. There were no hidden exceptions or troublesome hoops for customers to jump through to qualify for a replacement. We made the exchange process as efficient and straightforward as possible. Our object wasn't merely to sell Life Cycles but to hold on to our customers, because I knew what all business people know: it's a lot cheaper to keep an old customer than to find a new one.

Looking back, I can say now that our unconditional guarantee was a direct result of my experience as a consumer. I knew which businesses I was loyal to and why, and I wanted to inspire that brand of loyalty in our Life Cycle customers. To accomplish that goal, we committed ourselves as a company to customer service and customer satisfaction, and those practices and that attitude paid considerable dividends and were crucial to our success. Consequently, I'm more than a little surprised at the degraded state of customer care in business today, and many of the people I spoke with volunteered their own poor opinions of the increasingly common practice of cutting costs at the expense of good customer relations.

"We measure everything we do by the customer experience and the quality of our coffee," Howard Schultz clearly stated. "The battle cry of our company has to be *exceed the expectations of our customers and exceed the expectations of our people*. It's about one customer and one cup of coffee at time. When we're at our best, that's what we're focused on." Schultz went on to name Costco as a company he admires for their abiding devotion to their customers. "They're one of the best managed companies in America," he said. "Costco's whole business philosophy is based on providing their customers a great value. No matter the cost of goods, Costco's margin is always 8%. They are relentless for the customer. They stick to their purpose, no matter how successful they become."

Ray Thurston, whose career was built on engineering efficiency into complex business processes, shares Howard Schultz's view that compromising on customer service and customer relations, all in the name of cost cutting, isn't just short-sighted; it's starkly counterproductive. "The general attitude is 'damn the customer,'" Ray told me, shaking his head. "It's a case of businesses trying to make more money with less. I have a secretary, so if I have a problem with a product or a service, she can make the call and take the time to straighten it out. But what about everybody else? Bad customer service is expensive. The cost to us as a community is horrendous."

Worse still, a company that fails to treat its customers, clients, and vendors well is far too often a business that can't be bothered to treat its employees well either. So morale tends to erode, momentum stalls, and the organization generally sloughs off Cookie Lee's "what-are-we-trying-to-achieve-today" ethic. Nearly everyone I spoke with had seen some degree of this sort of thing play out in his or her own experience. Even the best businesses can lose their way, given the wrong leadership, the wrong luck, the wrong emphasis.

When I interviewed Howard Schultz, he had only recently returned to Starbucks after an eight-year absence. He contended that some bureaucratic ossification had set in while he was away. "Multiple layers of bureaucracy had sprung up in the company. It was impossible to get a feel for the customers. I was pleasantly surprised by the passion and enthusiasm people had once we started removing levels of. . . nonsense. We had come to feel like the government or a bank, and we're an entrepreneurial group of people. People lose the courage to be creative when they have to go through layers to get anywhere."

While bureaucracy in business can be beneficial in imposing order, it can also be more than a little deadening, particularly if you believe — as Howard Schultz does — that business success often relies on sound instincts and deft touch, on a willingness and an ability to improvise. "You can't teach feel and instinct and touch," Schultz said, "and this company has always had great touch."

So the question becomes what *can* you teach and, conversely, what can you learn? What I distilled from my past year of interviews is that the best CEOs and entrepreneurs share among them a knack for thinking like their customers. They are capable of seeing their businesses both from the bottom up and from the top down. They are incisive and instinctively diagnostic and never lose sight, on a practical level, of what makes business work.

Panda Express' Andrew Cherng needs, understandably, to be concerned with the cleanliness of his ever-expanding chain of restaurants across the country. His eateries are open for long hours in high-traffic locations like shopping mall food courts and airport terminals, so keeping them impeccably clean is a bit of a chore but also, in Cherng's view, an absolute necessity. Meeting community health codes isn't enough for Cherng. He expects his employees to surpass them. "We want our employees to clean their restaurants like a five-star hotel," Cherng explained, "but it's not enough just to ask them to do that. They might not know what I mean. But if I send them to a five-star hotel, then they'll know, so that's what we do."

Andrew Cherng is all about showing rather than telling. He believes deeply in touch and instinct as business necessities, and he was given throughout our conversation to couching valuable business principles in readily-digested anecdotes. "A friend of my father's had a Japanese sushi place in Encino," Andrew told me. "Every time they came to our restaurant, we bought them dinner. Every time we went to theirs, we paid. Today they have zero restaurants and we have 1,100. Which is better?"

When he started in the restaurant business with his father in 1973, Andrew Cherng ran the front of the house, and he discovered the value of building relationships with his customers. "Even after thirty-five years," he commented, "I can still remember customers' names. Who's getting married. Who's in the hospital. I would have been a very good gossip columnist. The intimacy with customers is very special." But that sort of interest, that compassion, can't begin and end with customers and clients. It has to extend to employees as well or it becomes hollow and hypocritical. It becomes unsustainable. Good businesses are built to treat their customers and employees in essentially the same way.

When I asked Andrew Cherng to define success, he responded in a fashion I'd come to expect, given the course of our conversation. "Success is in inspiring more people to care about the things I care about." The key word is "inspiring." "I once went to a parenting class," Cherng recalled, "and one of the messages I came away with was to treat my children like all of the people in the world, and treat all the people in the world like my children. At Panda Express, we believe in sharing and taking care of our people. We like being a private company. We'd like to stay private.

That way, we can afford to do the right thing the right way, and that's important."

In my view, the success of Panda Express is principle driven. Andrew Cherng and his wife and partner, Peggy, have managed to keep the company true to its roots as it has grown and prospered, and that's no easy thing. They've resisted the tendency in business to misplace the purpose and lose the thread. I think it's significant that two of the entrepreneurs I talked to — Howard Schultz and Mike Ilitch — had left their businesses, intending to retire, only to see them drift and flounder, and each man returned to right his ship.

Ilitch left Little Caesars in 1993. "When I hit 65, I wanted to turn the company over to the people who'd been loyal to me," he explained, and then went on to add bluntly, "It didn't work out." When I asked him why not, Mike shrugged and said, "I turned it over to three or four people, but there are only so many number ones. My wife and I didn't want to interfere. We let them go a little too far, and the business got hurt. We had to step back in and rebuild it."

When I asked Mike if he could explain the difference between his approach to running the business and the approach championed by the people he'd left in charge, Mike made it simple for me. "I'm a feel guy," he said. "I like to be out in the field. I'm not much for details. I depend on people to give me good numbers and give them to me fast. I learn a lot about business through traveling. I like to see what people are doing. Not just in my business but everywhere." Touch again. Instinct. Feel. Qualities Mike's hand-picked replacements had either lacked or failed to rely on.

The Little Caesars veterans program, founded to help Iraq War veterans become Little Caesars franchisees, was a recent idea of Mike's and a quintessential example of his approach to business. He read a newspaper article about a wounded vet with poor job prospects and decided he could do something about it by supplying Little Caesars franchises at discount rates for vets. "It just felt right," Mike observed.

A good CEO or an inspired entrepreneur steers his business by his principles. Sometimes those principles are codified as company policy, but more often they're the underlying bones of the enterprise, the superstructure that holds everything else up and makes success possible. When the principles are sound, are honorable and sustainable, success follows.

In his book about his career at Starbucks, Howard Schultz laid out the guiding principle of the company he'd created as powerfully and succinctly as anyone might. "I wanted," he wrote, "to make Starbucks the sort of company I wished my father had worked for." Schultz's father was a janitor by trade and had spent his life working for businesses that cared little for his health or welfare. They could always get another janitor. Howard Schultz was inspired by his father's experience to take a different view of his responsibility to his employees. Having seen his father served badly, Schultz was determined to serve his employees well.

"Starbucks," Schultz told me with justifiable pride, "was one of the first companies in America to give health coverage to every employee, even part-time employees. There are lots of stunning stories," Schultz continued, "about people who've come to Starbucks as part-time workers who are now managing large organizations within the company.

They hired on wanting to be part of something larger than themselves and got caught up in the culture of the company. Like everybody else, our people are hungry to represent something they believe in."

So the job falls to Schultz and his colleagues in Seattle to hew to the guiding principles upon which the company was founded. "People measure our success in many different ways — stock price, competitive landscape, etc. Then there's success for 200,000 employees," Schultz clarified, "who we call partners. They're relying on me to preserve and enhance the integrity of this company. When I can look in the mirror and know we've done that, then I'll feel successful."

In Schultz's eight-year absence from Starbucks, the company didn't so much get away from its founding principles as stifle them with unnecessary layers of process and management. "People lose the courage to be creative when you have to go through layers to get anywhere," Schultz said. So his job, as he sees it, is to take the company back to basics — one customer and one cup of coffee at a time.

Of course, a large part of the fortunes of Starbucks going forward will hinge on its employees, and Schultz was quick to point out an employee-centric company he admires. "Look at In-N-Out," he remarked. In-N-Out Burger has been in business since 1948, and the company's drive-thru hamburger stands are confined to California, Nevada, and Arizona. The business was founded by Harry and Esther Snyder and was based upon the simple philosophy of giving customers "the freshest, highest quality food you can buy, and providing them with friendly service in a sparkling clean environment." The only changes through the years have been the addition of indoor and outdoor seating at some locations and the means for the employees, called associates, to have an ownership stake in the company.

"I'm amazed and stunned at In-N-Out," Schultz said. "It's extraordinary. You've never seen a cleaner bathroom in any restaurant in America. The secret is to treat your people better than you treat your customers. Employees aren't liabilities. They're assets."

In my experience, the belief that employees are assets is key to understanding how a company does what it does and why. If a business is indifferent to its employees, if it just sees them as replaceable cogs, what else is it likely to be indifferent to? Its community? Its customers? Its products? Just as with Starbucks and In-N-Out, these things are all tied together. That's why the inherent values of a company are key to its chances for lasting success.

When asked about his responsibilities as CEO of Oakley, Scott Olivett detoured into a more general discussion of leadership as a business virtue, a discussion centered upon values as a core business necessity. "A leader," he said, "needs to create a vision for the future. What are we that transcends our business objectives for next year? What are we instead of something that cranks out widgets? Organizations need a consistency of values. Everybody needs to be in agreement on what's important. This isn't necessarily about right and wrong. With values, there aren't necessarily right answers, and the mix varies from place to place. What organizations need fundamentally is consistency.

"Do we value coaching people?" Scott continued. "Do we value giving our own employees the first shot at opportunity? As leader, you have to decide on your philosophy and articulate it clearly, but only once you're ready to live by it. One of my guiding executive principles is that it's not about me," Scott added. "I've been in situations where decisions and the culture revolved around individuals, but I won't ask anyone to do anything I wouldn't do myself. If I'm going to ask somebody to be at the office all weekend to prepare for some rollout, I'm going to be there as well. We're all in it together. Team success rather than individual success."

Scott went on to tell me, "It's unlikely that a manager today will manage a homogenous group of people. Understanding and adapting around people is very important. One of the fundamental problems of business is that people now want more out of their work environment than they're getting. There's shortsightedness in business, driven by the markets, and that creates a disconnect. Even if you're not treating your employees well for compassionate reasons, the math of treating people in a short-term manner doesn't make good economic sense," Scott insisted. "You see less turnover in those companies that create a good working environment and are doing something their people believe in."

Almost without exception, particularly among the active CEOs I interviewed, employee turnover cropped up as the wrench in the system. The wealth of lateral movement within the business community is due in part to changing generational habits. With his large and relatively young workforce, Howard Schultz is in an ideal position to assess the trend. "In 1987," Schultz recounted, "we had eleven stores and 100 employees. Today, 16,000 stores and 200,000 employees." Bear in mind that the average age of a Starbucks employee is twenty-three. "Young people don't learn the same way we did," Schultz assured me. "They don't read newspapers or books. They read on the internet.

The resources a company needs to inspire people at that age are very different from what was needed in the past. Their tolerance and patience level is very low."

So young employees today require specialized training. Passing out the company handbook just won't do anymore. In return for the trouble and expense of that training, businesses are repaid with far less employee loyalty than was previously commonplace in the workaday world. This is due in part to changes in habits in the workforce, particularly among younger employees who are accustomed to a kind of workplace rootlessness.

In recalling his early years in business, Alan Schwartz said, "When I got out of school, taking a job was a life decision. Today, kids think in two-year segments, if they're long-term thinkers. Business is partially responsible for that. Businesses don't return the loyalty of employees. That may make life more interesting for young employees, but there's a lot of lateral movement today in business."

So a business' core values affect not just the tone and comportment of the enterprise but have a real impact on the practical costs attached to retaining a workforce as well. "The retail industry generally uses attrition as a mechanism to keep labor costs down and benefits down," Howard Schultz observed. "As a result, the turnover rate in the retail and restaurant business in America is 400%. So people are untrained and they don't have an emotional attachment and belief in what they're doing. The first thirty days of an employee's life," Schultz added, "are key. That initial imprinting process has to be conducted with respect and dignity."

In casting around for a culprit for the sizable turnover rate in the American retail and restaurant business, Schultz chose to lay a portion of the blame on the misplaced emphasis common to the academic business curriculum. "Business, as it's taught," Schultz observed, "spends a disproportionate amount of time on getting rich. If I were teaching a business class, I'd start off with what the values of the business are as opposed to what the profit potential of the business plan might be. If I were starting a business today," Schultz said, "the most important discipline I would identify would be human resources. Most emerging businesses get to HR last because they view it as a cost center. But the human resources director needs to report to the CEO."

It's all about the people, and any of us who have ever dealt directly with a business — which would be all of us — know that instinctively. An employee with both an interest and competence in what he or she is doing can defuse all sorts of thorny circumstances and put the company's best face on all dealings with customers and clients. An employee who treats each job as if it's temporary, and behaves accordingly, can do disproportionate damage to the business that employs them. So just as it's up to every company to imprint its values on its employees with the dignity that Howard Schultz referred to, the employees need to reciprocate — even if the job is likely to be short-lived, as many jobs are these days.

A good employee embraces the employer's values, which means it's incumbent on anyone applying for a job to know what they are getting into. The advice of Pat Fuscoe, mentioned earlier, applies doubly here. "Center yourself on something you believe in," Fuscoe tells young workers. "Don't be mercenary. Do what you do because you believe in it. Find something you're emotionally aligned with, and that will lead to a more productive career."

Given that we all need to eat and pay the rent and that none of us can really afford to wait around for the perfect slot at the perfect company, it may take you a few tries to land a job that's well aligned with your sensibilities and core beliefs. But landing that job should be your goal, because it's upon such jobs that productive careers are built. In the meantime, let honor reside in making the very best of the job you have. Take Wing Lam's example to heart. "I've always tried to improve every job I've had," he remarked. That is truly in keeping with the entrepreneurial spirit. How, the entrepreneur asks, do I make this work better? A process. A service. A technology. A job. The same question applies to all.

I doubt there would be fifty Wahoo's Fish Taco restaurants scattered across the country if Wing Lam hadn't devoted himself early on to being the best dishwasher, the best busboy, the best waiter. If he hadn't committed to the perfection of the task at hand, no matter how inconsequential and menial that task might have seemed. Wing was determined — as we all should be — to let his principles, his values, shape the work rather than the other way around.

Now back to Cooper, the Great Dane from Grand Rapids. The reason Cooper's story resonates with Howard Schultz is that it illustrates a full penetration of the core values of Starbucks from the boardroom to the drive-thru. Cooper's cup of whipped cream, given spontaneously and regularly by the employees of this Michigan Starbucks, is business precisely as Howard Schultz wants it to be practiced. If, as Schultz insists, Starbucks measures everything they do by the customer experience and the quality of their coffee, then Cooper and his owner are the fruits of that metric. Their treatment and their loyalty is

Shultz's goal on a global scale. That's why Howard Schultz has a photograph of Cooper the Great Dane in his office, and that's why he should.

The other side of the coin looks something like this. A couple of years ago, when ALS began to rob me of my ability to walk, I bought a specialized power chair called an ibot. The chair was developed by Dean Kaman of Segway fame, and it promised to make the world more accessible to wheelchair users through revolutionary technology. The ibot came equipped with tandem wheels that could swivel and rotate in such maneuvers as to allow the user to climb and descend stairs. Better still, gyroscopes helped to raise and balance the chair at human eye level height for face-to-face conversations. There was nothing else like the ibot available, and I wasn't about to let the $25,000 price tag stand between me and cutting-edge technology.

In many respects, the chair lived up to its promise, but there were a few flaws in design and build quality that left my experience as a user far from perfect. Given my background in the design and construction of exercise equipment, I had some ideas about improvements for the ibot. I had even tempted a few colleagues to work on the chair in a bid to improve the overall function. I went so far as to imagine the good people at Johnson & Johnson, who were marketing the ibot, might find my detailed opinion of the chair — both its virtues and its faults — valuable and useful.

Accordingly, I took the time and trouble to write a very explicit seven-page letter describing my experience with the ibot. I gave an account of what had broken and why, suggested a few remedies, and sent the letter off in the spirit of constructive criticism. I was a disgruntled customer only to the extent that I wanted the chair to be better, to be more reliable, which I assumed was what Johnson & Johnson wanted as well.

Their response, after some weeks, was a figurative pat on the head. I was offered a princely $400 discount on my next $25,000 ibot, and no attempt was made to address any of the issues I'd raised. Johnson & Johnson effectively responded to my letter by yawning at me. That is a choice businesses make at their peril.

Today I have a new wheelchair. It is not an ibot. Johnson & Johnson's web site indicates that no chairs have been sold after January of 2009. The ibot is no more. I can only guess why.

It could be that no one knows better about the importance of mobility in the lives of disabled people than Ken Behring, who talked to me about the life-changing experience he had in Romania, lifting an elderly paraplegic man from his bed of rags into a new wheelchair. "I was so profoundly affected by the overwhelming feeling I got when that man, who had just lost his wife, grabbed my hands to thank me," Ken tried to explain. "He had tears running down his face and was so elated because now he could go outside his home, he could visit neighbors, because now he had freedom."

Ken and his sons run The Wheelchair Foundation with much the same rigor and forward thinking as his previous careers, partnering with Rotarians around the world to raise funds and deliver wheelchairs. He admitted to me that nothing compares to the feeling of someone's new-found happiness when they receive a wheelchair.

"It's amazing to think that just about $100 can provide this kind of impact and change a person's life," Ken confided. "To think that it can make the difference of whether a person feels like they are whole, whether they want to live or die. You can't put a price tag on that feeling of helping people."

Ken is now working with the Lion's Club organization on funding cataract surgery for elderly people worldwide. "For the first time, they can see their grandchildren," he beamed. "And that is very emotional for me because I know how much this means to them."

Whether for-profit or not-for-profit, every business is only as good as its customers' and clients' happiness. That happiness is built on principles and values that need to be pervasive throughout an enterprise to be worthwhile. How you do what you do matters, no matter who you are or where you fit — from executive vice-president to barista-in-training. The golden rule of the Old Testament — treat others as you would have them treat you — is alive and well in every successful company. In the businesses that thrive, in the ones that last, honor matters. So be conscientious. Be principled. Always be honorable.

Lesson Five:

Always Be Compassionate

As I write this, leaders of our nation's financial industry are taking a well-deserved flogging both in the press and before Congress. To judge by the evidence, the mortgage end of the banking business has been a special offender in this most recent housing boom by choosing to champion fees over due diligence, avarice over responsibility. Bad loans — what we all now know as "toxic assets" — were underwritten, bundled up, and sold off at what has proven to be extraordinarily inflated prices. Clearly, these bankers were far more interested in the revenues generated by these loans than the fundamental integrity of them. They were only conscientious about their greed, not about their customers. Not about their communities. Not even about the institutions that employed them.

The reckoning is still unfolding. It promises to be far reaching and catastrophic for many. While the potential remedies are the subject of hot debate among our political leaders, the cause for the crisis is conspicuous and easy to explain. The bad paper is just a symptom. The failing was far more elemental and human. The people who made this mess either forgot or chose to ignore a fundamental principle of good business that is key to good living as well: we are all in this together.

A business that treats its customers as marks and its associates as patsies is sure not to last. Just look how far these banks have fallen in so little time. They've lost not just their good reputations and gobs of money but the sympathy and allegiance of their customers and the trust of their shareholders. The failing, flailing banks have been guilty of a far-ranging multitude of fiduciary sins, but they are unified in their wholesale lack of perspective. In this particular calamity, the hunger for profit eclipsed decency and good sense. The answer to Cookie Lee's habitual question — "What are we trying to do today?" — should never be, "Make as much money as possible, no matter what."

Based on my experience as a chief executive and my conversations with CEOs and entrepreneurs, I can say with certainty that good business citizenship is more productive and more sustaining for any company, no matter its size, than a relentless and naked drive for profits can ever be. Community — and their place in it — was very much on the minds of everyone I interviewed. The notion of treating customers and clients as prey was entirely alien to them, and though the banking crisis was still on the horizon as I travelled the country interviewing business leaders, I can readily imagine how appalled the men and women I talked with must be by the revelations of the past few months.

I remember in particular a story Glen Tullman told me. "I went on this website the other day," he said. "It's called Donors Choose, and I'd gone there because I'd gotten a $50 credit from Crate and Barrel. It turned out to be a site for requests for donations. A schoolteacher, for instance, might write in because she needs a table for kindergarteners or basketballs or books or something. You can make specific contributions for each request, and I was soon up to $3,500. The question I'm left with is how could we possibly have come to the point where teachers have to go on the internet to buy stuff like this?"

The current financial crisis serves as a partial answer to that question. In an earlier chapter, Scott Olivet of Oakley referred to the problem of misalignment within companies. The banking fiasco suggests that misalignment across an entire industry is also possible. All executives, management, and employees have to do is forget what they're supposed to be up to. Forget the fabric they're a part of, the community they belong to. "I think what you do for your community is part of the measure of success," Alan Schwartz told me, and his opinion was widely shared among the people I talked with. Certainly businesses exist to make money and realize profit, but they can't exist only for that. "In our business, we believe in tithing," Alan said. "Philanthropy tells you something about the soul of a company. It takes your eye off the bottom line a little bit, and we think it's a more rewarding experience when not only are you making money but you're giving back as well."

For five years in Chicago, Alan's tennis clubs provided teaching pros for the city's nearly seven hundred public tennis courts. The work was done pro bono, and under Alan's leadership, the monies charged for the use of courts in the more affluent parts of the city were spent to repair courts in the poorer areas. The benefit to the city was substantial but so was the benefit to Alan's company — not necessarily in profit but in civic-minded morale. The effect of a business doing selfless, compassionate work for its community frequently rebounds to the employees in the form of justifiable pride and boosted morale.

As Scott Olivet noted previously, most everybody in business is looking to be a part of something bigger than themselves. Organized philanthropy within business — encouraged compassion — provides an outlet for everybody's best impulses. "Giving makes us better for it," Scott declared. "If I try to convince you academically that philanthropy is great for your progression in your career, you're going to do it for the wrong reason. Better if I invite you to a charity event. If you get it, great. If you don't get it, maybe you should be doing something else with your time."

Oakley hosts and sponsors an annual event known as The Snowball Express. "We invite the families of fallen soldiers [from the wars in Iraq and Afghanistan] to Oakley and try to have them experience something they wouldn't get anywhere else. We bring in every athlete we can get to be there, and we invite all of our action sports athletes — skateboarders, skiers, etc. In our first year we had fourteen X Games gold medalists in the parking lot. They were signing autographs and doing exhibitions.

"It's great for the kids — not just to see the athletes but also to bond with other kids. They've grieved with their families but probably not with other kids in the same situation. We want them to know we care about them. We want to do something special for them. The whole event is touched with sadness and happiness at the same time. It's one of those days." Commenting on the impact on Oakley's employees, Scott added, "We turn away volunteers. Last year, we had seventy-five percent of the company volunteer for the event."

Compassion, at bottom, is all about looking out rather than looking in. While Scott and I were talking, I couldn't help but notice him sizing me up and soaking in my condition, my power chair, my failing voice, the paralysis in my extremities that is one of the symptoms of ALS. "How can I be here with you today," Scott acknowledged at last, "and not think about my life differently?"

Ken Behring also commented about my physical challenges being "unfair" because he believes that people who have worked hard should enjoy what they've created in life. He was, however, dismissive of any conversation about his own retirement.

"My philosophy about retirement is never retire," he remarked. "I'm 81 and working harder today than I've ever worked in my entire life. But now my time is spent giving back and helping people. Everyone should learn to show kindness because there's such a need in the world."

Ken's company is currently working in China (which he referred to as the New Frontier for developers) to build senior communities in much the same way he built clustered neighborhoods here in the states. His plans will bring relief and a new way of living for millions of elderly now in high rise buildings with no elevators.

"We're developing communities with activity centers, exercise facilities, and gardens for flowers and food," he explained. "Undoubtedly, I'll make a lot of money but I will also be giving it back to the Chinese people." He has already built seven museums for China, developed roads and bridges, and serves as a Board member for China Disabled to help the 83 million in that country who suffer with physical disabilities.

Compassion — both on a corporate scale and as a personal impulse — hinges on our ability to think about our lives differently. The vibrating base note of compassion is empathy, and Glen Tullman told me a story that put empathy in perspective as a virtue, not just in life but in business as well. "One of our senior vice presidents has a son with epilepsy," Glen said. "He was doing a bike ride to raise money for the disease, and I asked for a copy of the list to see who from our company had donated. Some employees were upset, but I told them, 'It's a free country. Work wherever you want. I want to see the names.'

"I wasn't interested in the amounts," Glen assured me. "I just wanted to see who the smart people were. I need to know who the giving people are in our company, because those are the people I want to promote. If you won't give to your boss, then you won't do anything for your clients or your customers."

Glen's message, in short, is that empathy and compassion translate. Our ability to put ourselves in the place of others — to think about our lives differently — affects how we do what we do. How we approach our work. How we deal with clients, customers, vendors, associates, and colleagues. It informs who we are by every practical measure. Compassion matters, and it isn't merely about money. More commonly, it's about time, which can be more difficult to give and is oftentimes more valuable. Time not just with charitable causes, but time with colleagues and clients and customers. The good business man or woman, the sort of employee Glen Tullman would want to promote, is the caring one who is frequently the smart one as well.

You don't have to be Gandhi or Mother Teresa to get ahead in business, but a solid sense of perspective is always an asset. The blinkered, purely self-interested employee is bound to be indifferent to context. His or her focus is so constricted that they may be tempted — even routinely tempted — to do something good for themselves that's not necessarily good for their colleagues or their company. A certain degree of selflessness isn't just good for the soul; it's good for business.

That brings me back to the current economic meltdown. It was recently revealed on the front page of *The New York Times* that investment banks, industry wide, paid out nearly $20 billion dollars in bonuses for 2008 — a year that saw a 35% depreciation in the value of the stock market and found many of these same institutions on the receiving end of tens of billions of dollars in government assistance so they might stay afloat. Even if we take into account the curious nature of Wall Street bonuses — as much compensation as perk — the fact that these banks chose to practice business as usual in the face of a plunging economy and their own red ink betrayed a colossal lack of perspective on their part.

The case of Merrill Lynch was particularly egregious. Merrill posted $15.3 billion dollars in fourth quarter losses in 2008, and yet CEO John Thain saw fit to pay out $4 billion in bonuses to his colleagues and employees, and he lobbied Bank of America executives — BofA had only just acquired Merrill on the cheap — for a $40 million bonus for himself. A just reward for his stewardship, he claimed. Thain's case was hardly helped by the news that, while Merrill was sinking, he spent $1.2 million renovating his office, a makeover that included a Pentagon-worthy $1,400 wastebasket.

The national contempt heaped on Thain and his colleagues was most succinctly voiced by the junior Senator from Missouri. "These people are idiots," Claire McCaskell announced from the well of the Senate. No argument here, given the circumstances, but I think a qualification is in order. The prevailing criticism of these "idiots" is and has been organized around their greed. At a time when national unemployment is crowding double digits, homes are being foreclosed on in record numbers, and the government is embarked upon a trillion dollar bailout of what, by any accounting, has been a flagrantly irresponsible financial sector, it's pretty easy to pummel Thain and his colleagues for their myopic avarice.

It seems to me, however, that the trouble isn't so much their greed as their selfishness. Lavishly paid investment bankers are nothing new. Neither are extravagant bonuses and even $1,400 trash cans. The difference this time is the dire national climate and bank executives' general unwillingness not just to be curbed by it but to even acknowledge it. When we bear in mind that the country's financial problems can largely be laid at the feet of these people, their eagerness to clamor for outsized compensation is little short of staggering and should be embarrassing to them. That it isn't tells us just how far they are from thinking about their lives differently.

The national fiscal pie is in such a shaky, diminished state that executives demanding their outsized slice of it seem self-involved to the point of childishness. These are precisely the sorts of people Glen Tullman would not promote, or even hire for that matter. "For too many years," Glen described, "business people have been measured by what they get. We need to measure them by what they give."

Glen has come to this view relatively recently, and he can trace the change in his philosophy to a particular moment in his life. "I had sold my second company, Enterprise Systems," Glen said, "and the sale had worked perfectly for everyone involved. I was invited by my alma mater, Bucknell, to speak on entrepreneurship, and I was feeling pretty good about that. I gave my talk, and afterwards

I was visiting with one of my former professors, Doug Canlin, who's an authority on primates. When I was in school, Doug taught me to speak and think critically and to write.

"Doug asked me, 'How do you think you're doing?' I told him, 'I'm doing pretty good.' He said, 'I don't think you're doing that well. In fact, you're one of my biggest disappointments as a student. We didn't educate you to make money. We educated you to make a difference, and I haven't seen it.'"

Glen confessed to being stunned. "That was a turning point in my life," he observed. "My brother's daughter had just been diagnosed with diabetes, and I'd sent in money and cared deeply about her, but that was the extent of my involvement." After his conversation with his former professor, however, everything changed. "I joined the Board of the Diabetes Foundation, and I was the only person on it without a child with diabetes. People thought I was a good guy, but I wasn't a good guy. I just had a good mentor.

"You get busy and get on this treadmill — you're going from one thing to another, and it's easy to forget how important it is to take time to give, because it always comes back to you," Glen explained. "I think my professor is much happier with me now. And I'm much happier, frankly."

Today Glen owns up to being a little extreme in his appetite for good works. "I've gotten more and more radical about the concept of giving back," he confessed. "Charity is all about a few people making an enormous difference. In our company, we pay our employees to volunteer. They love that this is what we do. Each year, I give more than 100% of my salary. We've told our children we're not leaving them anything." Glen admitted that his children took the news a lot better than he would have.

"My mother cursed me in a positive way by telling me you never say no when asked," Glen said. "Of course, she also told me if somebody knows you gave, it only counts half." Glen took that as his cue to drop the talk of giving and just go on living the life of it.

"When you give something to somebody else as a kind gesture with no strings attached and no expectations, that's true friendship," commented Ken Behring. "I've reached out to poor countries, to disabled people, to seniors with cataracts, and to children who would never be able to visit a wilderness like Africa except in a museum that I built for them," he said. "And this has been such a joy for me, but also this has come back to me in ways so far above and beyond what I have given."

In my experience, the compassionate impulse is a kind of muscle. The more you use it, the more you want and need to use it. Wing Lam's account of how he got involved in doing things for others is particularly instructive because Wing's version of charitable work involves more in the way of time and resourcefulness than money. "Years ago, a customer asked for a little help with a walk-a-thon," Wing recalled. "I knew at some point the people involved would have to eat and drink, so I did what I could to help." Now Wing calculates he spends half of his time on charity and half on business. If Wing's hard-working philanthropy is a boon to the restaurant chain that he and his brothers run, Wing has yet to find a way to calculate the effect. "I can't measure the impact our philanthropy has had on the stores," Wing pondered. "There's no direct bounce back, but my brothers understand it's the right thing to do."

124

Wing feels, in fact, that it's such the right thing to do that he confesses to being mystified by those companies that fail to practice charity in any sensible and organized way. "In all the years that I've done this," Wing told me, "you'd think my competitors would catch on. For instance, when I cook for these parties on the beach, everybody else just sends coolers of food. It's okay, but it's not like smelling it cooking. I've negotiated all of my budgets with my vendors so we'll partner in philanthropy. I don't take the rebates from them. I have them give it to charity and let them take the credit for it. At the end of the day, I need to justify to the partners where our resources went and why, but I always try to give people what they want. I want to be able to call them next year and have them come back. The hardest thing to do is ask people for money, so we try to be smart about it."

What I noticed in talking to Wing is the pleasure he takes from this facet of his business which, in truth, isn't business at all. "I have a lot of fun with philanthropy and always try to partner up with people who genuinely want to make a difference," Wing explained "Sometimes a celebrity will just show up at an event for a few minutes and then leave. That's not right. If I see somebody at an event who is enjoying himself, I seek him out because I need to know that guy. The Vegas people want to know who the whales are. I need to know who the whales are for charity. I need to find guys who think like I do. I don't need to know the people who just show up. I need to know the players. I don't care if I sold one taco today if I just met a guy who thinks like I do. If I can find, each day, one more guy I can harpoon, I'm happy."

Of course, nobody starts off as a whale. For Wing's part, he began by giving what he had — food, time, and a talent for cooking. Initially for Wing, charity was grilling tacos on a beach. What he found there was a strain of pleasure and satisfaction that has become a principal motivation of his life. It's okay to start small. What's imperative is the willingness to see your life differently.

Steve Burd, from his perch as CEO of Safeway, has a slightly different perspective on institutionalized compassion. While Wing has yet to be able to measure the effect of philanthropy on the Wahoo chain, Steve Burd can readily detect the effects of Safeway's charitable efforts on the company's relationship with both its vendors and its customers. "At Safeway, we're always trying to figure how to do charity smarter and better," Steve asserted. "We approach it like we approach our business. We want to reinforce the free enterprise system, which has allowed us to achieve all we've achieved, and we feel like we have an obligation to pay back."

To Steve Burd's way of thinking, Safeway provides its customers and vendors the opportunity to participate in a highly efficient and well-honed charitable strategy that's very likely not available to them where they work or worship. "Once our vendors know about the breadth of our philanthropy, they think we're a good investment," Steve said. "They trust us to take care of their money. That's why we're going to get support when others might not. As for our customers," he added, "we want people to know what we stand for; that way, they'll participate more."

In one sense, Safeway's philanthropy is inseparable from its business model, but in a more practical sense, the company's charity can only be sustained if the distinction between business and philanthropy is always strictly observed. "We never twist a vendor's arm for business,"

Steve promised. "They come to us." It's the consistency and dependability of Safeway's commitment to helping others and improving the communities in which they operate that cements the relationship the grocery chain enjoys with both its suppliers and its customers. "Companies that can stop giving during hard times haven't allowed giving to become part of the fabric of the company," Steve determined. "If giving is part of the corporate culture, it's difficult to stop it. A company that just writes the check can stop when they need to hit their number. That really hurts the charities. They depend on that money."

Steve's experience with philanthropy at Safeway has informed his perspective on giving generally. "Americans," he told me, "are more generous than anyone in the world, and yet our respect on a world scale is probably at its lowest point. Part of the reason might be because we're just writing the check. It's the nature of the philanthropy that has to do with its staying power."

It might be better, then, to start out lacking the resources to write the check. "For younger people," he suggested, "I think it's important to give their time. Then as they get older, they'll already have experience in giving back. I don't know why service isn't embedded in the curriculum of every school," Steve added. "We want to get P.E. in the school system. Why not service?"

It's a good question. Why not service? We learn a lot in this life about taking and having. An education in giving should be just as easy to come by, and the time is certainly ripe for it. "Kids are about now, right now," Pat Fuscoe observed. "They want desperately to know that they're significant now and not spend a whole lifetime investing in something so they can be significant when they're dead.

They're ready to devote a good part of their time to something meaningful."

In the present economic climate, the opportunities for giving — especially for volunteering — are almost limitless. Even those people unwilling to think about their lives differently may, in this downturn, meet with the occasion to have to. "People are always going to fail," San Diego's Father Joe Carroll assured me. "It's called the human condition. If and when they do fail, is there someone there to help them come back? That's the question."

In business, as in life, perspective matters. Having your bearings, cultivating a sense of where you are and where you're headed, is sure to make a difference both in the texture of your life and the arc of your career. Simple human compassion should be as natural to us as breathing. Let's hope the fact that it isn't speaks more to the clutter in our lives than the nature of our intentions.

To the extent that caring about those around us lifts our gaze, it's a very good thing. If it also helps us progress more successfully in life and in business, then it's a necessary thing as well. Stay awake to possibility. Open your eyes, and open your heart. Always be compassionate.

No Thank Yous

Curiosity. Persistence. Strategic thinking. Honor. Compassion. These are the ingredients of success. What I recognized by accident thirty-odd years ago, when rank desperation drove me to give my exercise bikes away, has stayed with me throughout my career and into my illness. We are most certainly bound together, and only superficially in a web of obligation. We need each other to thrive, to succeed, and to be sustained as a society. These are the principles of life, and they should never be left outside the office door.

As we've seen in these pages, time and again, enduringly successful companies are united in their passion for doing the right thing the right way. The CEO and his colleagues in the executive suite may set the course, but the employees sail the ship. Everyone needs to be attuned and engaged, from the top dog to the lowliest intern. Good business is about paying attention to the details — and the details are not just profits but customers and clients and vendors and associates and decency and integrity and dependability.

Juxtaposed to the greed and self-focused business decisions of certain corporate executives, who in many ways hastened this country's economic tailspin, is the recent outpouring of compassion and giving when natural disasters occurred across the globe. Ken Behring, who has himself given more than $100 million to charitable causes, wisely called it "true friendship" when you give without expectation of receiving back. In this open gesture of giving, Americans have shown genuine friendship to people in the Philippine Islands, in the demolished cities of Haiti, and in the earthquake-damaged areas of Chile.

As a nation, we put aside our own financial troubles and donated money, time, and supplies to help those who face the devastation of nature's most brutal forces. Celebrities mobilized and hosted charity concerts, companies donated millions in support funds and relief supplies, and families across this country wrote generous contribution checks even as their own bank accounts are in distress. We have proven our ability for compassion and for true friendship, evidence of deep participation in the global web of connection with other people. This reflects our greatest potential. This is reciprocity at its finest.

I'll close with a story Allscripts CEO Glen Tullman told me. It's one I'll long remember. While a student at Bucknell, Glen was hired by one of his professors to travel out to his weekend farmhouse in the Pennsylvania uplands and clear the driveway of snow. He started down by the road and shoveled his way up toward the house. "By the time I got to the top," Glen explained, "I realized there was livestock up there, and I had no idea what to do with them." Glen hailed from the New Jersey suburbs. He didn't know from a barnyard. "The Amish neighbors started showing up," Glen said. "They'd heard I was there, and they came to help. They began taking me back to their farms, and I became fascinated by their culture, by their willingness to drop what they were doing to help somebody else."

Naturally enough, Glen was grateful for all of their assistance. "I used to thank them," he continued, "and they'd tell me, 'Don't say thank you — this doesn't end here.' For the Amish, a favor isn't a transaction. They were all about building a web of connections."

Glen ended up writing his post-graduate thesis on his experiences with the Pennsylvania Amish. Fittingly, it was titled *No Thank Yous.*

"What," Glen asked rhetorically, "is a social anthropologist who lived with the Amish doing running a technology company? Fair question. It's never about technology. Just like an iPod is about having music and being able to share it, technology is always about the chain, the connection, the impact." It is always, in short, about reciprocity.

It is far better to have a life rich with such connections than one merely peppered with transactions. It would seem that the best thing any of us can do for ourselves and our careers, from beginning to end, is to pay attention and leave ourselves open to the welcome surprise of thinking about our lives differently.

I'm reminded once more of Howard Schultz's guiding philosophy. "Everything," he is fond of saying, "matters." If nothing else, I hope this book has given you reason to believe.

Acknowledgments

Several hundred years ago, Ben Franklin hit upon "turning on the lights" in life. My reference, however, is a key idea that came to young Ben long before his accomplishments as an inventor and diplomat. As a teenager, he determined who he wanted to become by observing successful people and determining which qualities were worth emulating.

In much the same way, I encourage people to take inventory of characteristics they most admire in their associates. Be observant, make a list, and incorporate them into play for yourself. With a little practice, you make them your own, and the practice will become habit forming.

I would first like to thank all of the interviewees who took time out of their chaotic schedules to sit down and share with me their philosophies about reciprocity and the difference this makes.

Heartfelt appreciation for my wife, Lynne, and our children — Austin, Danielle, Lindsay, and Nicole. Without their extraordinary support and love, my journey would never have been possible.

To a rediscovered college friend, Anne Marie (Lippert) Taylor, for her invaluable advice, editing skills and hard work.

I would also like to take this opportunity to thank everyone at the MDA, especially Jerry Weinberg, Kevin Moran, Shannon, Gretchen, and Kelly.

And for the myriad of others, family and friends, who encouraged me and helped shape my vision of this book. Pages will be turned; the computer screen on which this was written will blink and fade; but it is my hope that the indelible mark of life's poignant lessons, as revealed in my conversations with some of America's most successful entrepreneurs, will find a way into your soul.

If a lifetime is measured by the depth and breadth of human relationships, then I am certainly a very blessed man.